In *Like Our Father*, Christina Fox equ[...] glorious task of leading children to k[...] has a rhythm: biblical principles dire[...] reflection on how those principles sha[...] our practice, which leads to application of those principles to real challenges. The chapters close with questions for further discussion, and a helpful prayer in light of the character of God. Before you wade into the ocean of how-to guides, read this book that reminds you of Who is parenting with you.

STEPHEN T. ESTOCK
Coordinator, PCA Discipleship Ministries (CDM)

Christina Fox is a wise mother, a gifted counselor, and a dear friend. Every time I pick up one of her books, I know it will be filled with the kind of biblically sound teaching and practical application that has served so many of her readers through the years. If you are a parent looking to learn from our perfect, heavenly parent, Christina Fox is sure to be a trustworthy companion and helpful mentor.

MEGAN HILL
Editor for The Gospel Coalition; author, *Patience: Waiting with Hope*

Our Father, who art in heaven, help me parent these kids! Every parent knows that in order to raise healthy, loved, and spiritually mature children, we need a parenting coach. In *Like Our Father*, Christina Fox reminds us we already have one—our heavenly Father! You'll walk away from this book with a fresh awe for the way God has lovingly cared for you and deep wisdom to help you raise your children rooted in His love. This is a parenting book I will read and reread.

ERIN DAVIS
Writer, Bible study teacher, and mother of four boys

Christina Fox doesn't just offer a parenting "how to" manual, but instead paints a beautiful picture of how our heavenly Father parents us, slowly shaping us into a conduit of His love and grace as we learn to parent our own children in His strength. Lay down the heavy burden of needing to know "how" to be the parent you long to be and soak in the pages of this book, which will draw your eyes upward to know and rest in the One who has everything you need.

SARAH WALTON
Coauthor of *Hope When It Hurts* and *Together Through the Storms*

This book surpasses parenting how-to guides, giving us practical wisdom to nurture kids in gospel truth. Christina Fox faithfully points us to the perfect parent: God Himself. Get ready to see what it means to imitate our loving Father and proclaim His beloved Son to our children, fully relying on His abundant grace.

BARBARA REAOCH
Author; former Director of the Children's Division at Bible Study Fellowship International

In a world full of prescriptive strategies that don't go the distance, *Like Our Father* offers an invitation to discover the "why" of parenting instead of the "how." Understanding the multidimensional glory of God as Father shapes both parent and child toward the ultimate aim of parenting—being more conformed to His image.

KAREN HODGE
Coordinator of Women's Ministries for the Presbyterian Church in America (PCA) and author of *Transformed: Life-taker to Life-giver* and *Life-giving Leadership*

Simply put, *Like Our Father* is an excellent resource for parents who want to understand how our status as adopted sons of God helps us parent our own children. By inviting us to experience how God parents us, and then demonstrating how our sonship informs raising our children, Fox teaches readers how to image God's father-love in our families. Parents will fall more deeply in love with our heavenly Father and with the children He has graciously given us to raise.

ANNA MEADE HARRIS
Editor-in-Chief, *Rooted Ministry* blog, and cohost of the *Rooted Parent Podcast*

LIKE
OUR
FATHER

HOW GOD PARENTS US
AND WHY THAT MATTERS
FOR OUR PARENTING

CHRISTINA FOX

MOODY PUBLISHERS
CHICAGO

Published in association with Don Gates, THE GATES GROUP—www .the-gates-group.com.

A version of the section "Our Unchanging Father" was previously published at the author's website, christinafox.com.

Edited by Amanda Cleary Eastep
Interior design: Kaylee Dunn
Cover design: Erik M. Peterson
Cover illustration of leaves copyright © 2020 by milezaway / Shutterstock (1243120687). All rights reserved.
Author photo: Your Spirit Photography

ISBN: 978-0-8024-2442-6

Originally delivered by fleets of horse-drawn wagons, the affordable paperbacks from D. L. Moody's publishing house resourced the church and served everyday people. Now, after more than 125 years of publishing and ministry, Moody Publishers' mission remains the same—even if our delivery systems have changed a bit. For more information on other books (and resources) created from a biblical perspective, go to www.moodypublishers.com or write to:

Moody Publishers
820 N. LaSalle Boulevard
Chicago, IL 60610

1 3 5 7 9 10 8 6 4 2

Printed in the United States of America

To my parents,
who first introduced me to my Father in heaven

CONTENTS

INTRODUCTION

I still remember the day we brought our first child home from the hospital. He was five days old and had already endured a difficult delivery following a category 3 hurricane that brought our seaside town to a standstill. I had complications following his birth, so we stayed at the storm-damaged hospital for a few more days while we both underwent tests and visits from multiple specialists. Friends and family came to visit and reported the wreckage Hurricane Jeanne left in her wake.

The morning the nurse came in and said I was ready to be discharged, I nearly blurted out, "Who says?" Those first few days of parenting had already left me feeling like a failure; what would happen once we were set free from the safety of the hospital where knowledgeable staff appeared at the click of a button? Wouldn't it be safer to just remain there?

My husband carefully placed our nearly ten-pound son in his blue plaid carrier for the first time and buckled him in. As we walked down the hall toward the elevator, I kept turning around, expecting a nurse to come running down the hall to give us final take-off instructions. No one came. We left with nothing but the lingering promise from the nursing coach that she would follow up in a few days.

We arrived home to a yard filled with debris from the storm and a living room with stacks of boxes, packed with our most important belongings that we'd brought with us when we sought shelter during the hurricane. Our cluttered and disheveled home mirrored how I felt: like everything had been flipped upside down.

I looked at my son and then at my husband. "Now what?" I asked.

I asked the question most of us ask when we first become a parent: *What do we do now? Just how do we do this parenting thing?*

Those first few weeks (okay, months) we focused on survival. We were like a blind person stumbling about in unfamiliar terrain. Everything about parenting was new and scary and uncertain. We reached out and grasped at whatever we could find to lead us in the darkness. We had so many questions, many of which were left unanswered.

What I wanted most was for someone to come in and write out a step-by-step plan I could follow. While there were some helpful tools and resources available, I still felt uncertain. I often looked at my son and wondered, *Am I doing this right?*

These days, our children are older (and far taller than I!) but our parenting questions continue. Some days, the teenage years seem harder than those first days with our newborn. Often, parenting feels like the blind leading the blind. We still wonder: What should we do? Should we say yes to this request or no to that one? How do we respond to this situation? How do we help our teen navigate this challenge? Indeed, there are often more questions than answers.

Every parent has questions, and this book is about the questions we ask as parents; but as you'll soon see, its focus is on one important and foundational question. It is this question that helps shape how we respond to all the others. For that reason, this book is different than many other parenting books.

A Different Kind of Parenting Book

I don't know about you, but I have at least a dozen parenting books sitting on my bookshelves, and I've read many more besides. Maybe you have too. Each of these books provides methods and solutions to parenting challenges. They promote specific ways to parent children at different ages and stages. They include rules and checklists and anecdotes. They all seek to provide insight into the mysterious club we suddenly find ourselves in when our child is first placed in our arms at the hospital or at the courthouse following an adoption.

Some of these parenting books are written by seasoned parents who discovered an effective method for their three children and want to share it with us because, after all, if it worked for them, surely it will work for us too! Many are written by parenting gurus and professionals whose worldview is far different from ours, so we find ourselves weeding through the pages to find out what is true and helpful while setting aside all that is not. Others are written by medical professionals who throw around frightening statistics and warnings but provide little in the way of encouragement.

This book is a different kind of parenting book in that it is not a how-to book. There are not ten steps to follow. There is no list of ways to get your child to stop doing something. That's because this book isn't about techniques, strategies, or methods. I'm not a parenting guru. I'm not even one who has a personal method

I've used that I want to pass on to you. Instead, this book is about who God is, who we are, and how that gives form and shape to our parenting.

What to Expect

So, what can you expect from this book? You can expect to learn about God and yourself. You can expect to reflect on your relationship with God and what it means to you that He is your Father. You can expect encouragement from the gospel. You can expect to close the book at the end, refreshed from the glorious truths of how God works in your life. And you can expect encouragement and insight into imaging God to your children.

More specifically: Chapter 1 focuses on how we were created as image bearers and what that means for us in terms of who we are and our purpose in life. Chapter 2 looks at our adoption as children into the family of God and what a wonderful privilege it is to call God "Father." The remaining chapters look at specific ways God parents us and how, as image bearers, we can image Him in our own parenting.

We'll see how God is consistent in how He relates to us and what it means to image God as we are consistent with our children. We'll look at the boundaries and limits God sets for us and what it means for the limits we set in our home. We'll look at how God teaches us, disciplines us, and provides for us and what this means for our own parenting. We'll also look at God's love and patience for us and how we image those characteristics to our children.

At the end of each chapter, you'll find discussion questions for personal or group use. Consider meeting with a friend who is knee deep in the trenches of parenting and discuss each chapter together. Meet with a mentor, one who is further along on the parenting journey, and talk about what you learn. Discuss the book in a small group with other parents.

As a fellow parent, join me as we set aside all our how-to questions about parenting and consider the fundamental question: Who?

1

IN THE IMAGE
OF GOD

What is your most pressing parenting question right now? Whatever age and stage your child is currently in, you likely have a question at the forefront of your mind. A question that nags at you throughout the day. A question about what to do and how to do it. A question about how to help your child with something. A question about what to say yes to and what to say no to. Not knowing the answer likely leaves you feeling frustrated and helpless.

I don't know about you, but I've had questions about parenting since the moment my first child was born. Sixteen years later, the questions continue. These questions change with the child's age and stage, situation and circumstance, and even with what is going on in the world around me at the time. Often, I've wanted someone to step in and just tell me what to do.

Perhaps some of these questions resonate with you:

- When should I expect my child to crawl, walk, speak, or _____?
- How do I get my child to sleep through the night?
- What do I do when my child won't do _____?
- How do I talk to my child about _____?
- How do I help my child make friends?
- How do I teach my child to _____?
- Should I let my child _____, listen to _____, watch _____?

All parents have questions about raising children. I once had a job working as a counselor for families in crisis. One of my main tasks was to meet with families in their homes, observe the parents' interactions with their children, and then teach them parenting skills.

During our first few sessions, I liked to help these parents create a foundation upon which they could build their parenting. I wanted them to think through their purpose and goals for parenting. I wanted to help them see the big picture before we zeroed in on the specifics.

What I quickly found is that most parents did not want to look at the big picture. They wanted me to help address the current problem at hand. They often said things to me like, "Just tell me what to do when my son says _____ or does _____." Or, "Tell me what to do to get my daughter to stop _____." They wanted me to answer their most pressing question: How?

Fast-forward a number of years. I had my first child and found myself flipping through the pages of parenting books at the bookstore wondering the same thing those parents once asked me: "How do I get my baby to sleep longer stretches?" "How do I keep my toddler from touching things that can hurt him?" "How do I handle conflicts during playdates?" And most importantly, "How do I keep my patience in all the chaos?"

While just about everything in life seems to come with an instruction manual, our children do not. This does not mean people haven't tried to develop such manuals. Bookstores are lined with them. There are magazines focused entirely on parenting. Browse online and you'll find plenty of blogs providing how-to lists like "Ten Ways to Get Your Child to Eat Vegetables" or "Three Steps to Getting Your Child to Pick Up After Themselves." You know those blogs. You click on them in anticipation, follow the steps word for word, only to find that the solution simply did not work with your child. Or perhaps it was helpful with one child but not the other. Or maybe your child responded positively at first, but then the method fell flat and you were back to where you started.

Perhaps you've opened your Bible hoping for some parenting help but found little in the way of step-by-step instruction. There doesn't seem to be an answer to the "How?" questions of parenthood. That's interesting, isn't it? As much as we would like it to, we can't open the Bible and expect to find a verse or passage that says, "When your child will only eat chicken nuggets three times a day, do this: _____." Or, "When your child has trouble making friends in school, do these three things: _____." Or, "Two steps to get your child to say please and thank you." This is true for many things in life, including questions about employment and marriage and the future. That's because the Bible isn't a step-by-step manual on how to live life. It's the story of God's redemption for His people. It's the story of who God is and what He has done for us in Christ.

Yet don't despair, dear friend! God's Word does have things to teach us as parents. The Bible may not answer the question "how?" but it does answer the question "who?" God's Word teaches us

The Bible isn't a step-by-step manual on how to live life. It's the story of God's redemption for His people.

who He is and who we are, and these truths both have a significant impact on how we parent. While the Bible may not provide steps and procedures to follow, it does point us to truths that can shape the whole of our parenting.

Let's start exploring this question of "who?" by going back to the beginning, to the book of Genesis. There we'll get a picture of who God is and who we are.

In the Beginning

"In the beginning, God . . ." (Gen. 1:1).

As the first book of the Bible, Genesis lays the foundation for all that is to come. Its name is telling, for the word genesis means "beginning," and the book tells us how everything came to be. Moses wrote the first five books of the Bible to instruct Israel about the God who rescued them from slavery in Egypt. They had been in bondage for four hundred years, living in a land ruled by pharaohs and filled with idols to thousands of gods. They needed to know not only who God is, but who they were as well.

Genesis 1 and 2 recounts the story of creation—how God spoke this world into being, filled it with life, and placed humankind on it. Genesis 1:3 tells us God merely called forth light, and the light appeared; He spoke, and there it was. When we walk into a dark room, we have to toggle on the light switch before the lamp comes on. Yet, God, the Maker, speaks and all life appears *ex nihilo*, out of nothing. These beginning verses of Genesis are fundamental to our understanding of who God is: He is the Creator and sustainer of all things; He is the first cause to our existence. We are His creatures and are dependent on Him.

The creation account then tells us how God brought shape and form to the earth and then filled it with plants like grass, trees, and flowers, and with creatures like fish, birds, and bears. The Bible tells us the plants and trees were to sprout forth more plants and trees "according to its kind" (1:11). It also tells us that God made birds and fish and other animals "according to their kinds" (1:21). God then looked at His creation and called it good.

Then the Bible tells us about the creation of human beings. This account stands out from the rest of the creation story as something special and different:

> Then God said, "Let us make man in our image, after our likeness. And let them have dominion over the fish of the sea and over the birds of the heavens and over the livestock and over all the earth and over every creeping thing that creeps on the earth." So God created man in his own image, in the image of God he created him; male and female he created them. (Gen. 1:26–27)

Humankind stands apart from everything else God made because, unlike the rest of creation, we are made not according to an animal's kind, but in the image of God, the *imago Dei.*

This passage is significant, for it tells us of our inherent dignity, value, and worth. As the psalmist wrote, "For you formed my inward parts; you knitted me together in my mother's womb. I praise you, for I am fearfully and wonderfully made" (Ps. 139:13–14). God crafted us with His own hand and in His image, marking us as significant—not because of who we would one day become or what we would one day do, but because of who our Maker is. Every human life is valuable because we bear the image of God.

In God's Image

But just what does it mean that we are made in the image of God?[1] What does it mean to be created in His likeness? First, we were created as God's children. In Luke's gospel, he refers to Adam as God's son (Luke 3:38). Sinclair Ferguson points out that being a son of God and being made in God's image and likeness are interchangeable; they are synonymous.[2] He writes, "If we wish to understand what man was intended to be, we need to think of him as a son of God. If, in turn, we ask what it means to be a son of God, the answer must be found in terms of being God's image and likeness."[3] Ultimately, we see God's image in the person of His Son, Jesus Christ, who is the "exact representation of his being" (Heb. 1:3 NIV). When we want to know what it looks like to image God, Christ sets the standard. In the next chapter, we'll look more into what it means that God is our Father and we are His children. For now, though, let's continue to explore the significance of being an image bearer.

This passage in Genesis teaches us who we are and what our purpose is on this earth. We are God's sons and daughters. We are His image bearers; we were made to image and reflect our Maker. We were made to mirror God; we point to Him. The moon in the dark night sky has no light of its own; rather, it reflects to us the light of the sun. In a similar way, we image to the world—and to our children—who God is. As theologian R. C. Sproul wrote, "The task that is given to mankind in creation is to bear witness to the holiness of God, to be His image bearer. We are made to mirror and reflect the holiness of God. We are made to be His ambassadors."[4]

Further, as God's children, we glorify Him when we live our lives for Him. He made us and sustains us. He gives us life, breath, and everything else. Author Hannah Anderson explains that one result of bearing God's image is that we belong to Him: "He is tied to us. By placing His image in us, God assumes an extra measure of ownership and responsibility for our lives. We are His brand, His trademark."[5] We glorify God when we live our lives in dependence on Him, relying on and trusting in Him, rather than ourselves. We glorify Him when we return thanks for His goodness and kindness to us. We glorify Him when He is first in our heart, when He is our greatest joy and delight.

Have you looked up at the night sky with your child and marveled together at the sheer number of stars? They sparkle against the darkness of the sky. The psalmist wrote that the heavens "declare the glory of God, and the sky above proclaims his handiwork" (Ps. 19:1). When we look at what God created, we marvel at His handiwork, and He is glorified. Like the stars in the sky, we glorify God when we do things that make much of Him. We glorify Him when we display the wonders of who He is. We glorify Him when we worship and praise Him for who He is and all He has done.

Imaging God's Character

Many people say my youngest son is the mirror image of my husband, especially when we look at old pictures of my husband as a child. We often joke with our son about it. My husband will say to him, "Hey, how's my face doing today?" Or, "Look at my face. It'll be yours one day." My son laughs and embraces being my husband's "mini-me." In this way, my son represents his father. He is like him in terms of what he looks like. He also mirrors his father in his sense of humor. My husband and son often compete for the title of "Funniest Person in the Family." (To be honest, I always vote for my son!)

While we don't physically look like God because He is a spirit, our bodies do point to the power and wonder of God. The intricacies in how each part works together testifies to the creativity of our Maker. We also bear God's image in terms of who He is in His character and in what He does. And when we mirror Him, we live out our purpose and give Him the honor He is due. We show others who He is as we glorify Him. The Bible tells us this is why God created us, "everyone who is called by my name, whom I created for my glory, whom I formed and made" (Isa. 43:7). We don't make God glorious; He already is. Rather, we highlight and exalt who He is in His character, being, and works as we bear His image in the world.

God's Incommunicable Attributes

One of the key takeaways we learn from the creation account in Genesis is that God is the Creator; we are His creatures. He stands apart from us as the One who creates all things from nothing. He is the sovereign King and Ruler of all that exists. Nothing and no one can compare to Him. As Moses later wrote, "Who is like you, O Lord, among the gods? Who is like you, majestic in holiness, awesome in glorious deeds, doing wonders?" (Ex. 15:11).

When we consider the ways in which we image God in this world, we have to separate those characteristics that belong to God alone from those we share with Him. Theologians refer to the characteristics we do not share with God as incommunicable attributes. These are characteristics inherent to God and His divine nature.

For example, we are not omniscient. Only God knows all things. Because we are enfleshed beings, we cannot be omnipresent; that is, everywhere at once as God can be. He is all-powerful, self-existent, and eternal. And, as English pastor Arthur Pink noted, God has no needs.

> There was a time . . . when God, in the unity of His nature (though subsisting equally in three Divine Persons),

dwelt all alone.... There was nothing, no one, but God....
During a past eternity, God was alone: self-contained,
self-sufficient, self-satisfied; in need of nothing.[6]

This is hard for us as dependent creatures to imagine. We simply can't fathom what it would be like to have no needs, to be self-sufficient within oneself. We are born needy and dependent on others. Consider all our children need us to do for them! From the moment our children are born, they need us to feed and clothe them. We change their messy diapers, take them to the doctor for checkups, and put them to bed when they are tired. We are alert to safety concerns, buckling them up tight in their car seat and ensuring dangerous items are kept out of reach. We do these things because they cannot do them for themselves. Yet, even as children mature, they are still dependent on others. Even when they are grown and have their own homes and jobs, they will never be fully self-sufficient. They will still need the wisdom of others. They will still need help accomplishing tasks. They will still be dependent on God for their daily bread. This is true of all humanity, and this "needing" is what separates us from God.

In addition, God's attributes have no limits. As author and Bible teacher Jen Wilkin explains, "Everything that is true about God's nature and character is infinitely true. He is infinitely creative, infinitely sustaining, unlimited by time. God knows no limits on his presence, knowledge, power, and authority."[7] In contrast, we are limited by our humanity. Our knowledge on a subject only extends so far. Think of how many "why" questions our children ask and for which we have no answer! We are constrained by time and space. We might run a house or a business or even a nation, but our authority goes no further. When we consider God's incommunicable attributes, we are humbled by the truth that God is God and we are not.

God's Communicable Attributes

However, there are many characteristics and attributes of God that are communicable to us. These are attributes that originate in God and are shared with us. Throughout the Bible, we read of these attributes, often found in instructions or commands. For example, the apostle John teaches us that God is love, an essential attribute to His character: "Beloved, let us love one another, for love is from God, and whoever loves has been born of God and knows God" (1 John 4:7). God is love, and when we love others, we image God. In our acts of love toward others, we demonstrate that we know God and that we belong to Him. When we comfort our daughter after she's fallen off the swing at the park or when a schoolmate hasn't invited her to the party, we show her the love of God.

When we invent and create and problem-solve, we image the One who made us. When we speak with truth, we image the God of all truth. When we promote justice, we point to the God who is perfectly just. When we show up to work on time and labor hard for our employer, we image the God who first worked for us. When we show patience to our tired and whiny child, we reflect the patience God has for us. When we share and sacrifice for another, we mirror the God who sent His Son as a sacrifice for us.

As image bearers, we glorify God when we do what He does—when we image Him in His character, works, and ways. All of God's communicable attributes are available to us. However, we know we often fail to image Him. We don't love others the way God loves us. We don't have patience with our children. We don't sacrifice our wants for the needs of others.

What happened to God's image in human beings? Why doesn't all humanity live for the glory of God and image Him as His children in this world?

Redeemed Image Bearers

In chapter three of Genesis, Moses transitions from the story of creation to explain how we got to where we are today. We no longer live in Eden as our first parents did. Humanity does not enjoy fellowship with God by walking with Him in the cool of the evening, as Adam and Eve once did. Genesis 3 tells us that our first parents fell into sin by eating of the one tree in the garden from which they were forbidden to eat. Eve believed Satan's lie when he asked her, "Did God actually say, 'You shall not eat of any tree in the garden'? . . . . You will not surely die. For God knows that when you eat of it your eyes will be opened, and you will be like God, knowing good and evil" (Gen. 3:1, 4–5). When they ate the forbidden fruit, sin entered the world, and with it the death and decay of all things.

Everything changed for humanity on that fateful day. The ground was cursed, and, as a result, we get our food by the sweat of our brow. From then on, childbirth would bring great pain and every human would be born with a sin nature. Mankind was barred from the garden and could no longer be in God's presence. And the image of God in us was marred. It's still there, but instead of living for God's glory, we live for our own. We no longer do the things God does. We seek our own way. We hurt, lie, cheat, and steal. We snap at our children or put our wants and desires before their needs. We sin in our thoughts, words, and deeds. And rather than find our life and hope in God, we look to false gods and worship them instead.

But God.

These are two of the greatest words in all the world! Just as God sent Moses to rescue His people from Pharaoh, He sent a Redeemer to rescue us from sin. Jesus Christ, the eternal Son of God, left the royal halls of heaven and came to earth. He took on human flesh and fulfilled the promise God made to Adam and Eve in Genesis 3:15 to bruise the head of Satan. He came to defeat sin by living the life we could not live and dying the death we deserved. He came to remake us into people who can once again live out our purpose as image bearers on this earth. Through faith in who Jesus is and what He has done for us, we are set free from sin and are made new so that we can live our lives for the glory of God.

In fact, the very Spirit of Christ now resides in our hearts. He works in and through us, transforming us into the image of our Savior. He strips away the old, creating within us the new. We are redeemed image bearers who can once again image God as we were created to do.

Imaging God to Our Children

At the beginning of this chapter, I said that the Bible may not answer the question "how?" but it does answer the question "who?" So, who are you? Who am I? This is the most important question one can ask in life. The answer to these questions first lies in who God is. God is our Creator. He made us and sustains us. He created us with a purpose: to bear His image as His children in this world. As sinners saved by grace through faith, we are redeemed image bearers. We live for God and His glory.

But what does all this have to do with our parenting? What does knowing who God is and who we are as image bearers have to do with raising our children? How does the answer to "who?" impact our "how?" questions?

Because we are image bearers, we image God to those around us. We reflect Him to others as we do what He does and as we display His character in our lives. And who do we see most often in our day to day life? Our children. As parents, we are often the first glimpse they see of who God is. In our responses and actions, we point our children to the God who made them and saved them. When we image and reflect God's communicable attributes, they learn more of who God is. When we parent our children the way God parents us, they see God through us.

The more we take time to dwell on the character of God and consider the ways He has made us to reflect Him, the more it shapes how we parent. The "who?" inevitably shapes the "how?" As we move throughout this book, we will look at specific ways we can image God in our parenting.

In the next chapter we will dig deeper into how God parents us. We'll talk about our adoption into God's family and the privilege it is to call Him Father.

Questions for Discussion

1. Why do you think many of our parenting questions have to do with "how?"

2. Why is it important to know who God is and who we are?

3. Take some time to consider more about who God is. Read Exodus 34:6-8; Romans 11:33-36; and Revelation 4:11. What do you learn about Him?

4. Read Psalms 16:11; 27:4; and 42:1-2. What does the psalmist find in God?

5. How does knowing our purpose as image bearers transform how we live our day-to-day lives?

6. Read 2 Corinthians 5:21. What has Jesus done for us? What does this mean for us as we seek to glorify God with our lives?

7. What are some attributes of God you can image today as you interact with your children?

A Parent's Prayer

Father in heaven, I thank You for the gift of life. You are a marvelous Creator, and all Your works are good. Help me understand the significance of what it means to bear Your image in this world. Help me as I consider what it looks like to image You to my children. Be at work in me as I seek to glorify You in my parenting.

In Jesus' name, amen.

2

GOD OUR FATHER

What was your child's first word? Every parent looks forward to hearing their child's first words. There is even a dedicated space to record it in those baby books where parents document all the events of a child's first year.

Once our toddler begins making sounds, our anticipation increases. When little Emily babbles and points at something, we wonder: Is she trying to say a word? What is it? When little Josh repeats the same sound over and over, we go out of our way to decipher just what it is he is saying. We point to various objects or people and enunciate each word clearly and slowly, hoping he will copy what we say.

With both my children, I thought for sure their first word would be "momma" or at least "dadda." In English, "mommy" and "daddy" are among the most common first words children say.[1] With both my boys, I thought their first word would be "momma" because they spent so much time with me each day; or, perhaps it would be "dadda" because they were always so excited to see my husband when he returned home from work. Yet, this wasn't the case for either of my boys. My oldest son's first word took us by surprise when he pointed to a clock and said "clock." The first word of my youngest—today the athlete of the family—was "ball."

Though my boys did not say "momma" and "dadda" right away, they did soon enough. It is such a sweet and tender moment to hear your child call you by name—for them to identify you as their parent. To give voice to the fact that they belong to you and you belong to them. To call out for you when they need you— when they've fallen and hurt themselves or are scared in the middle of the night. Hearing your child call you by name: there is nothing else like it in the world. Though I have to admit, when you finally take a break to use the restroom, and immediately someone cries out "Mom!" or "Dad!" you might wish they didn't know your name after all!

As believers, we refer to God as our "Father." Just as our children ask us to feed them when they are hungry, we pray to our Father in heaven to ask for our daily bread. Just as our children call out to us when they need help, we cry out to our Father to rescue us from trouble. Yet, how often do we stop and consider the significance of the fatherhood of God? Why is He our Father? How does He father us?

More Than Just a Metaphor

The Bible uses many images and metaphors to describe God and how He interacts with His people. These metaphors often employ everyday roles, items, or experiences to help us understand something of the character of God. In Isaiah 5, God compares Himself to a vinedresser, tending to His vines (v. 5). We know God is not a vinedresser, but we understand the work of a vinedresser and can compare this work to the work God does in our lives. In Isaiah 64:8, God is described as a "potter" and we as His "clay." This is another metaphor we can understand; a potter shapes the clay for his purposes, just as God shapes our life according to His will.

The psalmist refers to God multiple times as a "rock," a "fortress," and a "refuge." We know God is not an actual rock or fortress, but we understand the metaphor is telling us that just as a fortress provides shelter from storms, so too does God shelter us from evil. We know we can run to Him for help and hope and safety. In the New Testament, Jesus also used metaphors to describe who He is and what He came to do. Jesus said He was the Bread of Life (John 6:35), the Light of the World (John 8:12), and the Vine (John 15:5). These are all useful images that help us understand who God is. Our God is so great and so complex, it takes countless words and images to describe Him.

One common metaphor for God is that of Father. We find it in both the Old and New Testaments. In the Old Testament, Father is primarily used in reference to God's relationship with Israel (Isa. 1:2–3; Mal. 2:10). In the New Testament, however, the name Father is most prominent as it becomes the way in which believers relate to God.[2] There are over two hundred references to God as Father in the New Testament.[3] Throughout the gospels, Jesus refers to God as His Father: "Father, the hour has come; glorify your Son that the Son may glorify you" (John 17:1). He also taught His disciples to refer to God as Father: "Pray then like this: 'Our Father in heaven, hallowed be your name'" (Matt. 6:9). Several of Paul's letters stress our relationship with God as one of sonship.

Yet when the Bible uses the word "Father" to refer to God, is it simply a metaphor? Does the Bible use it to merely help us understand something about God because we all have fathers and know the role they serve in our lives? Or is the fatherhood of God more than a metaphor? Seminary professor D. Blair Smith argues that "Father" is more than a metaphor, it is God's *name*: "Scripture gives us a number of similes and metaphors for thinking about God's qualities, but we must recognize that it clearly and directly speaks of God *as Father*. What is more, Scripture reveals this is a personal *name*."[4]

This name, Father, is more than just an image or comparison to help us understand something about God. It is who God is to us.

This name, Father, is more than just an image or comparison to help us understand something about God. It is who God *is* to us. It denotes a relationship. It shows that we know Him and that He knows us. We belong to Him and He to us. My children call me Mom and my husband Dad because we are their parents and they are our children. There is an intimate relationship between us. Yet, only our children call us by those names. Even though I have a close relationship with other friends' children, they do not call me Mom. The same is true for God. Not everyone can call Him Father. Only God's children have this privilege. The Bible teaches us that we "become" children of God: "But to all who did receive him, who believed in his name, he gave the right to become children of God" (John 1:12). Something must take place in order for us to become God's children. That something begins with salvation, but it doesn't end there.

From Justification to Adoption

When we consider our salvation, we often focus on our justification; and rightly so, because it is what brings us into right relationship with God. In our sin, we cannot come into God's presence. He is holy and we are not. But through faith in Christ—in who He is for us in both His perfect life and sacrificial death—we are justified. God looks at us as though we never sinned; He accepts Christ's payment on our behalf. At the same time, Christ's perfect life is imputed to us, and we are wrapped in His robes of righteousness. We are now united to Christ. All that He is and all that He has done is now ours. This is the good news of the gospel. But it is not the end of our salvation.

Jesus did more than save us from the wages of our sin; He saved us *for* relationship with our triune God. Upon salvation, we are adopted into the family of God and become His children. Christ is now our elder brother, and all God's children are our brothers and sisters. In fact, this was God's plan from all eternity past, "He chose us in him before the foundation of the world, that we should be holy and blameless before him. In love he predestined us for adoption to himself as sons through Jesus Christ, according to the purpose of his will" (Eph. 1:4–5). How amazing is that! God loved us from before the foundation of the world. He chose us to be His children through the work of His Son, Jesus Christ. Our sonship is the goal and purpose of redemption.

On the night before He was betrayed, Jesus shared a final meal with His disciples and gave what is called the Upper Room Discourse. He told them what to expect when later He would be arrested. He promised them the Holy Spirit would come and comfort them. He taught them to serve one another as He washed their feet. Then He prayed a prayer for Himself, for the disciples, and for all those who would later come to faith. This beautiful prayer reflects Christ's union with the triune God and our union with Christ and other believers. It shows us how Jesus' work for us has brought us into relationship with the God of the universe. In part of the prayer, Jesus prays these words:

> "I do not ask for these only, but also for those who will believe in me through their word, that they may all be one, just as you, Father, are in me, and I in you, that they also may be in us, so that the world may believe that you have sent me. The glory that you have given me I have given to them, that they may be one even as we are one, I in them and you in me, that they may become perfectly one, so that the world may know that you sent me and loved them even as you loved me." (John 17:20–23)

Our salvation brought us into relationship with God. We see in this passage that Jesus is united to the triune God; we are united to God through the work of the Son; and believers are united to one another. God is now our Father through our union with Christ the Son. Further, this prayer tells us that in Christ, God loves us as much as He loves the Son. Think on that for a moment. The One who spoke worlds into being, the holy and righteous One who rules over all things, loves us as much as He loves Jesus Christ. What amazing grace! Consider the depths of love we have for our own children. It doesn't even compare with the love God has for us! Professor D. Blair Smith explains that because of this "gracious adoption, we share in an eternal, glorious relationship. Becoming a Christian, then, means coming into the Father-Son relationship."[5]

When people talk about what it means to be a Christian, they often refer to salvation from eternal punishment for sin. And it is that. But it is also much more. Being a Christian means becoming sons and daughters of God. It is about a relationship. A family relationship born of love. As the apostle John wrote, "See what kind of love the Father has given to us, that we should be called children of God; and so we are" (1 John 3:1). God the Father, through the life and death of the Son, and by the Spirit's regenerating work in our hearts, adopted us as His children so that we would join in the love and fellowship the Trinity has experienced together for all eternity.

Are you starting to see why the name "Father" is so significant?

Have you adopted a child or know someone who has? It is a beautiful real-life example of what God has done for us. I've walked with several friends through this process. I loved supporting, praying for, and encouraging friends as they labored to bring their adopted child home. One friend adopted a sibling group through the foster care system. It was a long and arduous time of waiting for the process to go through, but once it did, I was able to attend the proceeding at the courthouse. I watched as the judge declared that these children now belong to my friend and her husband. He officially gave them my friend's last name. It was a joyous and beautiful thing to watch! I don't think there was a dry eye in the courtroom. These children now call my friend Momma and her husband Daddy. They know all their needs will be met. When they are hungry, they are fed. When they are hurt, they are cared for. They are now part of a forever family.

This is true for us in our relationship with God. Our adoption into God's family makes us His sons and daughters. As Paul wrote in Galatians 4:4–7:

> But when the fullness of time had come, God sent forth his Son, born of woman, born under the law, to redeem those who were under the law, so that we might receive adoption as sons. And because you are sons, God has sent the Spirit

of his Son into our hearts, crying, 'Abba! Father!' So you are no longer a slave, but a son, and if a son, then an heir through God.

Our adoption enables us to call God, Father. It's what makes us His son or daughter. So, while our justification is what redeems us from sin, our adoption is what brings us into familial relationship with God. J. I. Packer, in his book *Knowing God*, argued that our adoption is the highest privilege the gospel provides.[6] He writes,

> In adoption, God takes us into his family and fellowship—he establishes us as his children and heirs. Closeness, affection and generosity are at the heart of the relationship. To be right with God the Judge is a great thing, but to be loved and cared for by God the Father is greater.[7]

Adoption may seem like merely a theological idea seated alongside words like atonement, justification, and sanctification. Yet, it is so much more than that! It is the beautiful and glorious truth that God loved us before the world began. He chose us to be His own, and then made us His own through the work of His Son. We are united to Christ, and His sonship with the Father is now our sonship. And because we are God's children, we have all the rights and privileges that come with it. Let's look at some of those benefits now.

Benefits of Being God's Child

There are many benefits to being a child of God, and throughout the rest of this book we will unpack a number of them. But for now, I just wanted to highlight a few. As you read each, take time to dwell on what it means to you that God is your Father.

We can come to God in confidence.

A remarkable thing happened when Jesus died on the cross; the curtain in the temple was torn in two (Matt. 27:51). This curtain separated the most holy place from the sanctuary. It symbolized the barrier separating sinful man from our holy God. But with Christ's final sacrifice, that barrier was removed. Through Christ, we can now come into the very presence of God. Not only that, but we can come to Him *boldly* and with *confidence*. We can cry out to God and know that He hears us. We can come to Him and seek His grace and help in time of need (Heb. 4:16).

I love how Tim Keller describes this confidence: "The only person who dares wake up a king at 3:00 AM for a glass of water is a child. We have that kind of access."[8] Think of how many times your child has called for you in the middle of the night. Perhaps she wanted a drink of water or just some reassurance after a frightening dream. And you gladly attended to her. We too have this access to our Father in heaven!

We can trust God to meet our needs.

We all have times in our life when we worry about our daily needs. We may worry about having enough to pay a bill that is due at the end of the month. We may hear rumors that job cuts are on the horizon and we fear losing our job. As parents, we often worry about whether or not we are meeting our children's needs. *Is Jack growing as he should? Is Kyra getting the education she needs, or should we advocate for assistance? Should I get Johnny the play-set all his friends have?* In Matthew 6, Jesus taught us that because God is our Father, we can trust Him to provide for our needs. He instructed us to look at how God provides for the birds of the air or the wildflowers in the fields. Jesus concludes, "Therefore do not be anxious, saying, 'What shall we eat?' or 'What shall we drink?' or 'What shall we wear?' For the Gentiles seek after all these things, and your heavenly Father knows that you need them all" (vv. 31–32).

Jesus used an argument from lesser to greater. If God provides for His creation (the birds and wildflowers), how much more so will He provide for His children? Our Father in heaven knows all our needs and cares. He knows them before we do! Consider all the ways you anticipate and meet your own child's needs. Often, parents can tell their child is sick before they even say, "I don't feel good." We always bring water and snacks for our children wherever we go. Just as we know what our children need and seek to provide for them, our Father in heaven does so for us.

We are heirs of God's kingdom.

As adopted children, we are God's heirs (Gal. 4:7; Eph. 1; 1 Peter 1:4). Everything secured for us by Christ is ours; nothing and no one can take these blessings from us: redemption, forgiveness of sins, sonship, the Holy Spirit and His work in us, our future resurrection, and all the glories of heaven. We receive all these blessings, not because of anything we've done, but simply because of who we are as God's children.

Consider the benefits your children enjoy by simply being your children. Think of all the things you do for them and the ways in which you provide for them. You save money to take them on a vacation or to put away for college. Every time they grow out of a pair of shoes, you take them shopping for a new pair—sometimes only a few months later! One day, they will inherit all you've labored to provide. How much more so are we heirs of all that God our Father owns!

God teaches and trains us.

God does not leave us as He found us. He not only saves us by grace and brings us into His family, He also teaches us how to live as His children. Through His Spirit, He works in us to make us into the image of His perfect Son, Jesus Christ. He trains us in righteousness. He helps us use our gifts for His kingdom. We might think of an adopted child who leaves behind an orphanage and a life of poverty to join her new family in their home. She is given new clothes. She learns the rules and ways of how they live. She receives a first-class education. She is provided opportunities to stretch her wings and try new things. Her parents provide whatever she needs to be successful in life. Likewise, God not only teaches us how to live for Him, He provides us all that we need to do so (2 Peter 1:3). He will finish His work in us, making us like Christ.

These are just some of the glorious truths and benefits we have as God's children. What a blessing and privilege to be God's own!

A Perfect Father

As you've read through this chapter and thought about what it means that God is your Father, pause to compare human fatherhood and the fatherhood of God. No doubt, our experiences with our earthly fathers likely have some impact on how we view our heavenly Father. While some of us may have fathers who loved and cherished us, others may not. Some of us may have fathers who went out of their way to disciple our hearts. Some may have fathers who listened to our fears, encouraged us in our gifts, and made us feel like we were valued and important to them. But others might have earthly fathers who were cold or distant. They might have fathers who were so busy and consumed with their own lives that they made little impact on their children's. Some might have fathers who were harsh or abusive. Others might not have known their fathers at all.

Whatever our experiences, whether positive or negative, we need to remember that God is a perfect Father. He stands far above any earthly father. Our fathers did the best they could in their fallen nature, but our Father in heaven only does what is good, right, and true. His love for us is unconditional, and nothing can separate us from Him. He never fails to provide for us exactly what we need. He is never neglectful of us. He may discipline us as needed (which we will look at in a later chapter), but He never punishes us, for Christ has born our punishment at the cross. He is the perfect teacher, the source and wellspring of all wisdom. Our Father in heaven is everything that our earthly fathers could not be. In fact, whenever we are uncertain what a good father looks like, we can look to the relationship between God the Father and His Son, Jesus Christ—the ultimate Father-Son relationship.

For those whose own fathers cast a dark shadow on fatherhood, let the rays of truth shine down on your heart. Take time to read and study what it means that God is your Father. Meditate on His great and perfect love for you in Christ. Consider the great lengths He went to in adopting you as His own. Dwell on the fact that He cherishes you. And like a child, run to Him. Cast your cares and sorrows on Him.

Imaging Our Father to Our Children

The purpose of this chapter was to help us explore just what it means that God is our Father. Our identity as Christians is fundamentally tied to who we are as God's children, made in His image and likeness. Just as my children are irrevocably part of the Fox family, we are forever a part of God's family. We belong to God and He to us. When we grasp this beautiful truth, it helps us begin to think about how God fathers us. And we will explore how He does so in the following chapters.

Let's now tie these first two chapters together and consider what all this means for parenting our children. In the last chapter, we looked at why we were created: to image and reflect our Father who made us. We image God by reflecting His character, works, and ways. In this chapter, we looked at the fatherhood of God. We are adopted children of the Father. God chose us in love to be His own. What a marvelous truth! It will take an eternity to plumb the depths of all the blessings we have as His children, but we touched on a few of those blessings in this chapter.

While we image God in many ways in our life and in a variety of circumstances, such as in our work, our creativity, and our love toward one another, one of the ways we image Him is in parenting our children. When we parent our children as God parents us—when we relate to them the way God relates to us—we show them who He is; we point them to their own Father in heaven. Imaging God to our children is an important privilege. To do so, we need to consider all the ways God parents us. My hope is that the following chapters will help you marvel even more at how God fathers you. And in turn, that it will open your eyes to ways you can mirror what God does for you in what you do for your own children.

Questions for Discussion

1. Do you know anyone who has adopted a child? How is it a picture of what God has done for us?

2. What does it mean to you that you are God's child? How is God your perfect Father?

3. Sometimes we forget or doubt our sonship. Read Romans 8:12–17. What role does the Holy Spirit have in confirming that we are indeed God's children?

4. What role does prayer have for God's children? How did Jesus teach us to pray?

5. Because we are united to Christ by faith, all that belongs to Jesus belongs to us. This includes His relationship with the Father. Read the following verses to see some of what Jesus has with the Father that is ours as well: John 12:26; 15:9–10; 17:14–19; 1 John 1:3.

6. In 1 John 3, we read some identifying features of God's children. What do God's children do?

7. What are some ways you can image your Father in heaven to your children today?

A Parent's Prayer

Abba, Father, what a privilege it is to call You Father! I come before You thankful for my adoption as Your child. I thank You for the sacrifice of Your Son to bring me into Your family. I pray Your Spirit would remind and confirm my sonship to me. Help me to never forget what it means that I am Your child and You are my Father. Open my eyes to see all the ways You tenderly care for me. And help me as I seek to image You to my children.

In Jesus' name, amen.

3

GOD IS CONSISTENT

Have your children ever reminded you of something you neglected to do, specifically something you always do but for some reason did not do?

From the time my children were babies, I read stories to them before bed. It was part of our nightly routine. Bath time. Teeth brushing. Story time. Prayers and hugs. Sleep. In the little years, these stories included *Goodnight Moon* and *The Going-to-Bed Book*. Sometimes read more than once. As they grew, the stories did as well. We read Bible stories and devotionals. Soon we added chapter books such as *The Hardy Boys* and *Tom Sawyer* and *The Hobbit*. It was a sweet ritual, and I cherish the memories of those times.

On a few occasions, we attended a special event in the evening or visited friends for dinner and returned home late. By the time we pulled into the driveway, at least one of the boys had fallen asleep in the car, head lolled to the side of his car seat. We quickly and quietly brought them inside and put them to bed, forgoing all the usual end-of-day rituals. We'd tuck them in, tiptoe toward the door, and then just as we'd start to shut the door, inevitably a little voice would ask, "What about story time?"

I would then walk over to his bed and try to explain that because we stayed out so late, we had to skip story time. Just this once. "We'll read extra tomorrow night," I'd promise.

It's no secret children find comfort in routine. They come to expect their day will unfold in a predictable way. Even more, they *need* structure and routine. From the time our children are born, pediatricians instruct us to establish eating, sleeping, and playing routines because children do best with predictable routines.[1] So, we create specific naptimes and bedtimes. We feed them at certain times of the day. We go to story time at the library every Tuesday at 10 a.m. Friday nights are for pizza and board games.

Children also develop their own routines that give order and structure to their day. For some children, this looks like drinking their morning milk while snuggled in your lap. For others, they might want to arrange all their stuffed animals in a row on the bed before their afternoon nap. Others watch the same cartoon program over and over without getting the least bit bored or insist on wearing the same red rain boots every day, no matter the weather. As our children grow, they might not necessarily require the same kind of daily schedule and they may stop carrying around their favorite fuzzy blanket, but they still need routines. They need structure and order for getting ready for school each morning. They also need to know what to expect from us when they ask, "Can I play video games this afternoon?" or what the consequence is for breaking a family rule.

In this chapter, we are going to look at the importance of consistency in our parenting—of developing regular and dependable routines, structure, and expectations for our children. But first, let's look at how the need for consistency points us to our Father who is consistent with us.

Our Unchanging Father

Inherent in the character of our heavenly Father is the truth that He does not change. "For I the LORD do not change; therefore you, O children of Jacob, are not consumed" (Mal. 3:6). This is hard for us as humans to understand. We change all the time. We change our mind. We change our preferences. We change hairstyles, jobs, and friendships. Even more, sanctification is all about change as we put off sin and put on righteousness. But God does not change. The same God who spoke and light broke into the darkness is the same God who rescued His people from slavery in Egypt. The same God who chose Mary's womb to carry our Savior is the same God who met Peter on the shores of Galilee and said, "Feed my sheep" (John 21:17). The same God who gave grace to David in his sin against Bathsheba is the same God who forgives us when we pray in repentance. The same God who rescued us from our sin at the cross is the same God who hears our cries for help today. Yesterday, today, and forever, God remains the same.[2] This is difficult for our finite minds to imagine; our eternal, unchanging God has always existed and always will.

This means that who He is in His character will never change. In Exodus 34, God greeted Moses with this description of Himself: "The LORD, the LORD, a God merciful and gracious, slow to anger, and abounding in steadfast love and faithfulness, keeping steadfast love for thousands, forgiving iniquity and transgression and sin" (vv. 6–7). No matter how many centuries pass, no matter the turmoil and chaos in the world around us, our God—*who He is*—does not change. Everything that is true about His character will always be true. That means we can trust our Father to always be steadfast in faithfulness, generous in love, and rich in mercy. He is always good and always does what it right and just. He will always respond to us out of this unchanging character.

Because God never changes, what He says does not change. Everything in His word remains true for all eternity. All that Scripture tells us about our world, our fall into sin, and what God did to save us, will never change. What the Bible tells us about who we are, what we need, and how God provides it, will never change. Whether or not people agree with what God's Word says has no impact, for it is firmly fixed forever. "Forever, O Lord, your word is firmly fixed in the heavens" (Ps. 119:89). Into all eternity, God's word remains: "Heaven and earth will pass away, but my words will not pass away" (Matt. 24:35).

This means His promises to us will never change. When everything in our life is flipped upside down, when it feels like we are riding on a fast spinning tilt-a-whirl, God's promises steady us in the tumult. Promises such as: "For I am sure that neither death nor life, nor angels nor rulers, nor things present nor things to come, nor powers, nor height nor depth, nor anything else in all creation, will be able to separate us from the love of God in Christ Jesus our Lord" (Rom. 8:38–39); "I am sure of this, that he who began a good work in you will bring it to completion at the day of Jesus Christ" (Phil. 1:6); and, "If we confess our sins, he is faithful and just to forgive us our sins and to cleanse us from all unrighteousness" (1 John 1:9). How many times have you promised your child something and then were unable to follow through? Not so with our Father. He will never promise something and fail to deliver on it. He will do all He says He will do.

A God of Order

Do you have a favorite season of the year? My favorite season has always been fall. I love the transition from hot weather to the chill of winter. I love watching the leaves slowly lose their verdant hue and reveal their true shades of crimson, gold, and burnt orange. I also love all the outdoor activities we enjoy in the fall: roasting marshmallows, picking apples, and navigating corn mazes. For many years, I lived in south Florida and missed watching each season transition from one to the next. A few years ago, we moved out of the Sunshine State. I've enjoyed sitting at my kitchen table and looking out the large picture window to the back yard, marveling as the seasons move forward from one to the next—of leaves changing colors, the winter winds blowing them away, and then the arrival of spring, as the new buds unfurl on tree branches until they are full of leaves once again.

This predictable pattern in the change of seasons speaks to something about who our Father in heaven is. Not only is He unchanging, He is also a God of order. When He created the world, He set in place laws for His creation. That's why the sun shines each morning and the moon lights our way each night. It's why summer follows spring and winter follows fall. It's why we know that everything that goes up must come down and how we know when to plant vegetable seeds for the garden each spring. It's why we know when children will start to crawl, then walk, then talk.

God also established rhythms for the life of His people. He set aside one day a week for rest. He instituted yearly celebrations for the nation of Israel including the Feast of Tabernacles and Passover. Jesus Christ established communion as a meal we share together until His return. We worship with our local church bodies every Sunday to celebrate our risen Savior. The Bible even reveals God's desire for orderly worship and provides for what to include in our services, including prayer, preaching, and singing praise to Him.

We also know God established specific laws and rules for His people. He told them what to expect when they broke the rules. He was clear about His expectations and equally clear about what they could expect from Him (Deut. 4). As a Father, He doesn't throw new rules at us out of the blue. He doesn't vacillate on whether something is wrong or not; if He says something is sin, it is always sin. He doesn't tell us to expect one consequence and then add a harsher consequence instead. His responses toward us are not impulsive or rash. We know what our Father expects of us and we can expect from Him in return. (We'll look at our Father's rules for us and His discipline of us in later chapters.)

In all these ways and more, God shows us that He is unchanging and that He values consistency and order. This means we know what to expect from our Father. We know that He will always relate to us in keeping with His character and His word. When we are worried or afraid, we know we can cry out to Him in prayer and that He hears us. When we have need of provision, we know we can ask for what we need, and He will meet those needs. When we require wisdom, we know He will provide it. When we endure a trial or hardship, we know He is with us and is for us. When we have fallen into sin, we know He will forgive us because of the work of Christ on our behalf.

It's such a comfort to think through all the ways God is consistent with us, isn't it? Life is often chaotic and confusing and uncertain, but knowing that God never changes anchors us. It grounds us in the everchanging circumstances in which we find ourselves. Knowing these truths about our Father gives us hope and peace because we know that He will never change in how He relates to us. He will always act out of His steadfast faithfulness, grace, and love. And because we know God values order and consistency, it helps us in our own parenting. It helps shape the way we engage with and respond to our children. When we are consistent with them, as our Father is with us, we image God to them.

Let's look at what such consistency might look like in our parenting.

Imaging Our Consistent Father

First though, you might be thinking, "But I'm not God. I'm not unchanging. I can't be consistent as He is." This is true. We are not unchanging. We are fallen sinners and prone to inconsistency. Think of the times you've set your alarm to rise early in the morning to read your Bible. It goes well for a few weeks and then you catch a cold. You sleep in for a few days because your body is healing, and you need the rest. Before you know it, you've gotten out of the habit of reading God's Word. This happens in many areas of life: diet, exercise, cultivating relationships, keeping organized with work, and more. We have good intentions toward consistency, but all too often we can't maintain it. It is also true that some people are naturally more organized. Following a routine comes easy to them. Others might be more spontaneous; schedules are difficult for them to keep.

Yes, we are not unchanging as God is, but we *are* redeemed image bearers. We know God is remaking us into the image of our elder brother, Jesus Christ. This means we are increasingly enabled to create order out of the chaos of life in this fallen world. This is what we do every day in our work. Whether we balance a business's finances as an accountant or prescribe medications to a sick patient as a doctor, we labor to push back the effects of the fall. It's what we do when we complete household chores, cleaning up messes, and putting away toys. It's what we do when we brush our teeth each morning, when we resolve conflicts with friends and family, and when we take our car in for repairs. Each act is a labor intended to rein in the chaos and brokenness and establish order.

As God's image bearers, we glorify Him when we create structure and order.

While we can never be perfectly consistent and while we will fail, intentionally or unintentionally, as God's image bearers we glorify Him when we create structure and order. We glorify Him when we seek to provide consistency for our children. We glorify Him when we develop a pattern or routine for the life of our family. What might consistency look like in our homes? How can we image our consistent Father to our children? Consider these areas:

Consistency in the Use of Time

As mentioned above, children perform better with a predictable schedule. Their bodies perform better when they get the same number of hours of sleep each night. Specific naptimes are helpful too, as well as eating, playing, and learning schedules. We all know what it is like when we have a busy day and we take our children from one errand to the next and before we know it, we've missed naptime. Or it's an hour past lunch. They start to deteriorate before our eyes. They lose all ability to manage their emotions. They start to whine or pull at us, dragging their feet throughout the grocery store. And we realize we pushed them too far.

When children know what to expect for the day, when they know what happens next, they know how to behave. Routines and structure help them feel safe; it reduces uncertainty which provides security. However, these schedules do not have to be rigid. If snack time is at 10:30 and little Sarah is hungry at 10:20, she doesn't have to wait ten minutes until it's time to eat. The idea of a daily schedule is so that everyone, both parent and child, knows what to expect for the day. There are certainly days when our schedules get interrupted. We live in a fallen world where people get sick, plans get cancelled, and an unexpected, urgent errand consumes our time. Such things happen and we need to be resilient enough to adjust when our life is interrupted.

On the whole, it is good for everyone to have a typical daily schedule. It will change as your children grow into different stages of childhood. (If you need help determining a good eating or sleeping schedule for your child, contact your pediatrician.) Naptimes will drop off. You'll add sports and other activities. Bedtimes will push back later and later—until you go to bed before they do! It is helpful for both yourself and your children that you post the family schedule where everyone can see it. If your children are too young to read, you can use images or drawings of what takes place throughout the day. At the start of the day, review with your children what will take place. Give them reminders before transitioning one from activity to the next. "In ten minutes we have to clean up the toys because it is Tuesday and we go to the library for story time on Tuesdays"; "Let's eat our lunch and then get ready for quiet time"; or, "Remember that I am picking you up early from school today for the orthodontist appointment."

Consistency in Our Responses

Have you had people in your life whom you never knew how they would respond to you? Would they be glad you called? Or would they sound irritated, as though you were an interruption to their day? Would they simply ignore and disregard you as though you were a nuisance? When we don't know what to expect from someone, it is disconcerting. We don't know how to approach that person. We don't know if they will be courteous or unkind.

With our children, the way we respond to them is important. Our children should know what to expect when they approach us. If sometimes we look at them and smile, but other times make them feel like they are a bother and an interference, they won't know what to expect from us. Like our Father in heaven, we want our children to approach us in confidence. We want them to know they are welcome. Even if they are interrupting us or catching us at an inconvenient time, we want to respond in a way that reflects they are valued and cherished.

Consistency in Rules and Consequences

We will discuss this in later chapters, but consistency in family rules and consequences for breaking those rules is also important. Our Father in heaven is clear and consistent with His children about His commands. He is also clear about the consequences for sin. Likewise, when we have consistent rules and consequences in our homes, we image our consistent Father to our children. This means if we tell our children they only have screen time on the weekend, we can't give in to their complaints and allow screen time on Wednesday afternoon simply because they are bored. If a ten-minute time-out is the stated consequence for taking a toy from a sibling, we shouldn't change it to thirty minutes in the heat of the moment. Or, if a child plays video games longer than the rule allows and the stated consequence is a reduction in play time the next day, taking away video game privileges for a month is not consistent. Such inconsistencies will only exasperate our children.

Consistency in Expectations

Have you ever had a job where you did not know what was expected of you? Perhaps you never received a clear job description. Yet, your boss made it clear when you didn't perform up to his expectations. This left you discouraged and frustrated because you never knew what was expected. But how could you possibly do what your boss expected if you were never informed of those expectations?

This is true for our children. We need to be clear about what we expect from them. Before we enter the grocery store, we remind them of how they are to behave. On the way to church each Sunday, we review how they are to participate in worship or Sunday school class. As we drop Johnny off at his friend's house for the afternoon, we have him recite to us the family rules about watching movies or playing video games with friends.

We also need to expect from them only what they are developmentally capable of doing. We can't expect a three-year-old to spend an entire day running errands without having a meltdown at the end. We can't expect our middle schooler to manage their homework schedule on their own if they've never been taught how to do so. As parents, we shouldn't be surprised by our children's immaturity, impulsiveness, curiosity, and disorganization. Children are still growing and maturing. We need to measure our expectations with where they are in their development.

Consistency in Rituals and Traditions

As mentioned, children adopt rituals they live by. Bedtime routines become sacred to them. Little Isabelle can't leave the house without her stuffed bear. We have our own rituals as well. Consider all that you do each morning to get ready for day. Check email and social media. Drink coffee. Listen to the news while getting dressed. Our habits and routines do more than shape our days; they also shape the direction of our hearts.

James K. A. Smith argues that we worship what we love, and our loves are shaped by our habits.[3] In essence, we become what we behold. The regular rituals, routines, and rhythms of our homes help form the direction of our hearts. We come to depend and rely on our habits to give our lives meaning. To give us hope in uncertainty. This gives us pause to consider the habits we live by and how they shape our hearts. Do they shape us to love God or what He has created?

We can use our children's natural desire for ritual and consistency to develop rituals that help direct our children's hearts to God and His ways. We can develop rituals and rhythms to teach our children who God is and what He has done—to create a household centered around worshiping Christ. The family dinner table can become a place of nightly worship as we give thanks for our daily bread, feast on the word of God while nourishing our bodies, and sing of His goodness to us as we share about our day with one another. Smith encourages families to incorporate music, story, symbols, and tactile objects to help children learn. "Children are ritual animals who absorb the gospel in practices that speak to their imaginations."[4] Family prayer time can consist of family members taking turns praying through cards on which are glued the faces of friends and loved ones or pulling out sticks from a jar with requests written on them. Consider ways you can develop daily rituals and activities that help your family keep their gaze fixed on Christ.

We can also use holidays and other special days to shape the direction of hearts. Lighting the annual Advent wreath, making handcrafted ornaments that tell the story of redemption, and singing Christmas hymns are all rituals that shape young hearts. All such rituals have an eternal purpose. They shape us to know and love our Savior. They also help us live out our identity as image bearers. As Smith writes, "We want to be *intentional* about the formative rhythms of the household so that it is another recalibrating space that forms us and prepares us to be launched into the world to carry out both the cultural mandate and the Great Commission, to bear God's image to and for our neighbors."[5]

Grace for the Inconsistent

Perhaps as you've read this chapter, you've thought of ways you've been consistent with your children and ways you have not. You are not alone! In my own parenting, I have days where I am consistent and days when I fall flat. Some days, I follow our daily routine. I am consistent with rules and consequences. I read our morning devotional at the breakfast table. Other days, it's like a free-for-all. Nothing happens as it should. I am distracted and forgetful. I respond to my children with irritation or sarcasm. Other things take priority. And in those moments, it is hard not to feel defeated in my parenting.

When we are inconsistent in our parenting, we must remember God's grace for us. We must remember that Christ is consistent for us when we are not. Our elder brother stands before our Father and intercedes for us. God looks at Christ and sees His perfectly consistent life lived for us. When we identify inconsistency in our lives, we can come boldly before our Father and ask for His help and wisdom. When our inconsistency is the result of sin, we repent and seek forgiveness. Then we get back up and start again.

Think of consistent parenting not as a rule that is impossible to keep, but as an *opportunity* to show your children who God is. Every time you are consistent, you image God to them. And when you are inconsistent, you have an opportunity then too—an opportunity to model what it looks like to appropriate the gospel to your life. In your weaknesses, you can show your children the grace of God. Tell them that it is hard to be consistent, but that you are praying for God to give you the strength to do so. Tell them all the ways God is always consistent with you. Teach them about their unchanging and consistent God.

Questions for Discussion

1. What does it mean to you that your Father is consistent? How does this impact your relationship with Him?

2. Read these promises from God's word: Matthew 11:28–29; Philippians 4:6–7; James 1:5; 1 John 1:9. What does it mean to you that God always keeps His promises?

3. Why is it hard to be consistent with our children? What areas are the hardest for you?

4. What are the expectations you have for your children? What can you do to make those clear to them?

5. What are some of your family rituals? How did they develop? Are they ones you want to keep? Why or why not?

6. What are some new rituals and rhythms you can implement in your home today that point your children to God?

7. How can you image your Father's consistency to your own children today?

A Parent's Prayer

Dear Father, I thank You for your consistent love and grace toward me. No matter how crazy life gets, I know You remain the same. You will always respond to me out of Your consistent character. What peace and security for my heart! I know I cannot be perfectly consistent with my children as You are with me, but I pray You would help me strive toward consistency. I pray they would see You through my consistent responses. May they see You through the order and routines of our day. Above all, may our family rituals help shape their hearts to love You.

In Jesus' name, amen.

4

GOD PROVIDES BOUNDARIES

When my oldest first started crawling around, I went to the store to find child safety gadgets. Mostly, I wanted to find outlet covers. I walked down the appropriate aisle and could not believe how many options there were! Door locks. Toilet bowl locks. Trash can locks. Covers for sharp edges of furniture. You name it, they carried it.

As parents, we want to keep our children safe from harm. Keeping them from sticking something metal into an electrical socket is a good thing. Preventing them from digging around in the trash can is just good for everyone. And for anyone who has an extra-curious child, a child safety cover for the front door handle can be a life saver!

These are boundaries we use to keep our children from harm. They are limits we put in place that say, "Don't go any farther," and, "This is not for you." But what about other boundaries? What about rules and limits? Are they necessary as well?

Depending on our own experiences with rules and commands, we may bristle at the idea of setting limits for our children. We may find rules stifling and limiting. We may even have past experiences with rules that were harsh and demanding. Or, on the other hand, we may put our hope and trust in rules, giving them more power than they deserve. We might expect rules and boundaries to rescue and save us and our children. To complicate things more, in our current culture, one person's rules might be different from another because there is no standard truth. This too can impact how we view rules for our children. Whatever our experiences with rules and whatever value they currently hold in our life, it is important that we have insight into it because it impacts the role rules have in our homes with our children.

As we'll see in this chapter, rules and commands are found throughout Scripture. We'll look at how God sets boundaries for us. God teaches us what is good and right and what is wrong and sinful. He says to us, "This is the way, walk in it" (Isa. 30:21). As we've seen so far, God is our Father and He knows what is best and right for us. He knows what is good because He is good. We will look at some of the rules and limits God has for us, what they mean for us, and how we can image God in the limits we set for our children.

God's People and the Law

In the first chapter, I mentioned Moses and how God used him to deliver the Israelites from slavery. Their ancestors were originally from the land of Canaan and left for Egypt because of a famine. Jacob's son Joseph had been sold into slavery and, through the providence of God, ended up in the employ of Pharaoh. God bless-ed Egypt through Joseph, who labored to collect and save enough food to last the nation through a famine. The rest of Joseph's family came from Canaan to join him. Because they were shepherds by trade, and thus detestable to the Egyptians, they settled in the land of Goshen.

Hundreds of years passed, various pharaohs came and went, and God's people grew in number. Egypt's king feared they would rise up against him, so he enslaved them and put them to work. They cried out to God for help and He heard them. He sent Moses to rescue them. Moses performed amazing miracles as God sent plague after plague against Pharaoh until he finally relented and let God's people go.

They began their journey away from Egypt and came to the Red Sea. Pharaoh had changed his mind, and his army was in hot pursuit. What would they do? Surely, they would die! God then did something remarkable: He opened the Red Sea so they could walk on dry land to the other side. When Pharaoh's army followed behind them, God folded the sea back down over them, killing both Pharaoh and his army. God's people rejoiced and praised Him for their deliverance.

As they traveled onward to the Promised Land, they continued to learn about the God of their fathers. After being enslaved for so long, they were used to the rampant idolatry of Egypt. They had much to learn about the one true God who rescued them. God showed them He was their provider as He blessed them with pro-visions in their journey: water from a rock and bread that appeared with each morning's dew, six days a week. Though they grumbled and complained and often wanted to return to what they knew best, God continued to provide and meet their needs. His pres-ence remained with them as He led them to their new home.

Moses then brought them to Mount Sinai. This is where they would learn who God is and what He expects from them. This is where they would learn what it means to be God's people. This is where they would learn how to be separate and distinct from the nations around them. This is where they would learn about God's best for them.

God's people were told to stay away from the mountain and to not even touch it. Moses climbed to the top of the mountain to meet with God and the people stayed in the camp below. They could hear the thunder and lightning from the mountain. They trembled in fear as it shook. But Moses remained on the mountain and received the Law, etched in stone by the very hand of God.

The Law, what we call the Ten Commandments, instructed God's people in how they were to relate to God and to others. The first four commandments spoke to their relationship with God. They were to worship Him alone, honor His image and name, and set aside one day a week for rest and worship. These commands taught them that God is God alone; there are no other gods. In addition, they taught the people that God was to be worshiped a certain way; He was to be honored as first in their lives. The rest of the commandments taught them to honor their parents, respect the dignity of human life, keep their marriage vows, respect their neighbor's property, speak the truth, and not envy one another. One day in the distant future, Jesus would be asked which of these is the greatest command. He would respond, "You shall love the Lord your God with all your heart and with all your soul and with all your mind. This is the great and first commandment. And a second is like it: You shall love your neighbor as yourself" (Matt. 22:37–39).

God also provided a list of rules which separated them from the other nations and rules for how to worship Him. There were rules for dealing with injustice and crime. Rules for how and what they were to eat. Rules for making sacrifices for sin. All these rules taught God's people who God was and who they were as His children. These rules revealed the holiness of their one true God. Because they were sinful, He also provided a way for them to pay for breaking these rules through the sacrificial system. The ceremonial laws were extensive and an entire tribe, the Levites, were tasked with ensuring proper sacrifices were made for the people's sin.

If you've ever read through the book of Leviticus, the sheer volume of commands can be overwhelming. I've often wondered how God's people remembered all those commands! And as we know, they could not keep them. That's why they needed a Savior.

It's why we need a Savior too.

Jesus and the Law

For centuries, God's people made sacrifices for their sins. The smoke billowing out from the temple never ceased. Animal sacrifice could never make full atonement for their sin. It merely acted as a temporary stay until a complete sacrifice could be made. Until the Redeemer came.

Jesus came as the perfect law keeper; He came to fulfill the law on our behalf so that He could then become the perfect sacrifice for us. In the Sermon on the Mount, Jesus proclaimed, "Do not think that I have come to abolish the Law or the Prophets; I have not come to abolish them but to fulfill them" (Matt. 5:17). In the rest of His sermon, He got to the heart of the commands. He taught that not only is committing murder sin, but so also is hating a brother in one's heart. He taught that not only is adultery sinful, but so also is lusting after someone else. In so doing, He showed us that the commandments went further than outward actions, but to our very heart—to our thoughts, desires, and motives. That's because our sin doesn't originate outside of us, but from within us. We are sinners and need limits and boundaries in order to live for God and His glory.

On this side of the cross, Christians often wonder what the laws in the Old Testament have to do with us. Because Jesus kept the law for us and sacrificed His life for us, do we still need to keep God's law? The Reformer Martin Luther taught that the law serves to show us our need for Christ. It drives us to the gospel because when we read God's law, it acts as a mirror revealing the sin in our heart and pushes us to Christ in repentance and faith (Rom. 3:20). I once had a college professor say that you can't read the book of Leviticus and not see Christ. That's because, in reading it, we realize the depths of our sin. We realize there is no way we can possibly obey God and live a perfect life. We need a Savior.

In addition, because we are fallen and prone to sin, the law helps to restrain sin. By having laws and consequences for breaking them, it keeps us from being as sinful as we could be. As much as we'd like to think that people will do the right thing, that we don't need rules to govern us, we know otherwise. Do you remember the first time your child told a lie or flat out disobeyed? It wasn't something you had to teach your child to do; it was inherent in their sinful nature. Without limits we will do what comes naturally. Laws and rules bring order to our world.[1]

Though we no longer keep the ceremonial laws because Christ is the final sacrifice for sin, we are called to follow after Christ. We are called to live like Him.

For believers, God's laws and rules also helps us understand who God is and what is important to Him. As image bearers created to live for His glory, we need to know what glorifies Him. When we read God's word and His commands, we learn what is pleasing to Him. We learn what brings Him honor and praise. Though we are not held to the old covenant as Israel was, and we no longer keep the ceremonial laws because Christ is the final sacrifice for sin, we are called to follow after Christ. We are called to live like Him (1 Cor. 11:1; Col. 1:9–12; Eph. 5:1–2). We are called to be like Him.

Obeying God's Rules in Light of the Gospel

Our obedience to God's commands is rooted in Christ and the gospel. When we read the New Testament, we come across many commands and admonitions. These rules and instructions teach us how we are to live for God as Christians. These admonitions are never listed on their own but are always tied to the truths of the gospel, of who Christ is and what He has done. Theologians often refer to these foundational gospel truths as "indicatives." An indicative tells us what God has done for us in Christ and who we are as a result. What then follows are the instructions or commands, what theologians call "imperatives." An imperative tells us how to live out these truths. The imperative is rooted in the indicative. For example, Ephesians 5:2 tells us, "And walk in love, as Christ loved us and gave himself up for us, a fragrant offering and sacrifice to God." We are called to walk in love (the imperative) because of what Christ did for us in His death on the cross (the indicative).

This is important for us as we read Scripture. When we come across an instruction for us to follow, we have to remember its tie to the gospel. We obey God's rules because of who Christ is for us. We obey God's commands in and through Christ. He is the source of our obedience. God looks at Jesus' perfect life lived in our place. He sees Christ's righteousness and not our sin. He accepts Christ's payment for sin as though we paid it ourselves.

What amazing grace! Through faith in what Christ has done, we are wrapped in Christ and His obedience. We wear His robes of righteousness. We obey out of love and gratitude for this amazing grace. But there's even more grace! We've received the gift of the Spirit. He is at work in us, helping us put off sin and put on righteousness. He works in our hearts, giving us a love for God's law so that we desire to obey it.

As we looked at in chapter 2, we are God's children, adopted in love before the foundations of the world. Our Father is a good Father and His limits for us are good. They are also for our good. They help keep and restrain us from sin. They show us who He is so that we can honor and glorify Him. They show us how we can image Him. And they show us just how much we need a Savior.

For Christian parents, we should understand the place of God's laws and rules in our lives. His commands for us play a significant role in our own rules for our children. They help us see the importance and necessity in setting limits for our children, for in doing so, we point them to God.

Setting Limits for Our Children

After forty years wandering in the desert, God's people were finally ready to enter the Promised Land. In the book of Deuteronomy, Moses prepared them to enter. He reminded them of everything they had learned about God and themselves. In Deuteronomy 5, he reviewed the Ten Commandments with them again. Then he taught them the importance of passing on what they learned to their children:

> "And these words that I command you today shall be on your heart. You shall teach them diligently to your children,

and shall talk of them when you sit in your house, and when you walk by the way, and when you lie down, and when you rise. You shall bind them as a sign on your hand, and they shall be as frontlets between your eyes. You shall write them on the doorposts of your house and on your gates." (Deut. 6:6–9)

Moses exhorted God's people to teach their children who God is and what He had done. They were to teach them what it looks like to love Him with all their heart, mind, soul, and strength. They were to teach them God's law, and not just once, but all the time and everywhere.

I remember as a new mom reading this passage and thinking through just what it looked like to teach my son who God is and what He has done every day, all throughout the day, and everywhere we go. This passage became the hinge for discipling my children. It helped me see that God is not compartmentalized to one area of life; He *is* our life.

As believers, we need to teach our children who God is, what He expects from us, and what it looks like to live for Him. We do this when we image God in the limits we set for our children. Having rules and boundaries is important. Our children need to know what is good and right to do and what is not. They need to know what is safe and what is harmful. They need us to point them to the narrow path of life and to warn them about what happens when they wander off the path. "In the path of righteousness is life, and in its pathway there is no death" (Prov. 12:28). God's Word teaches us the way to this path, and He calls us to teach our children as well.

We learned that one of the uses of God's law is to restrain sin. Like us, our children are born sinners, so they need rules and limits to help restrain their sin. This is why we don't let them steal a friend's toy during a playdate. This is why we teach them to use their words when they are frustrated rather than yell out in anger. As parents, we also know what is good and best for them. We know what is harmful and what is not. That's why from an early age we don't let them touch a hot pan and why we make them hold our hand when we cross the street. That's why we don't let them eat what they want when they want or watch television all day long. Because we are all born in sin and have a fallen nature, if we have no rules or boundaries we will follow the desires and passions of our sinful heart. This is true for our children as well. They need us to set limits for them because they can't do so for themselves.

Just as God does for us, we also set limits and rules to help point our children to their Savior. We teach them what God expects of them. We teach them His commands from Scripture. We teach them to obey God by obeying us. We teach them what glorifies God. But in so doing, we also teach them the gospel. We teach them who Christ is, why He came, and how His life and death paid for our sins. When they fail to obey, when they cross over the boundaries we've set, we show them how much they need Jesus and forgiveness for sin. We use rules and limits to help them learn to run to the cross and receive the free gift of God's grace in Christ. We also model this ourselves when we repent for our own sin.

Not All Rules Are Good Rules

But we must be cautious here; it is not just having rules that glorifies God, for not all rules are the same. The Pharisees had many rules, but they did not glorify God. "Woe to you, scribes and Pharisees, hypocrites! For you are like whitewashed tombs, which outwardly appear beautiful, but within are full of dead people's bones and all uncleanness. So you also outwardly appear righteous to others, but within you are full of hypocrisy and lawlessness" (Matt. 23:27–28). The Pharisees added to God's laws. They added rules and boundaries beyond what God stated, to the point that these rules became a heavy burden for the people. These rules are what we call "legalism" today. Modern legalism is not just additional rules and boundaries, but includes those times when the Bible's imperatives are presented without the indicative.

When my children were young, I'd drop them off to play at a friend's house and say something like, "Be good!" It sounds like a good thing for me to say, a reminder for them to not break the rules and risk not being invited back. But as we know, because of our sin nature, no one is good. When I tell my children to be good, it implies they are capable of doing so on their own, apart from the work of God within them. Further, if they are capable of being good, they have no need for a Savior. Perhaps I should have given them an imperative linked with the indicative: "Remember to love your friends as God has loved you."

Legalism produces hypocrisy. Legalists focus so much on their own rules, they fail to do what God calls them to do. This means we have to be careful that the rules we set are godly rules. Our rules need to be consistent with God's rules and seek to glorify Him. This might mean evaluating our own hearts and asking, "Is this rule for God's glory or for my comfort?" It might mean asking ourselves, "Is this about me and my convenience or about what my child really needs?" It might mean considering our motives: "Did I implement this rule for the sake of appearance because I care about what others think?" Some rules are unnecessary and rather than help our children, they only aggravate them. Paul cautioned against this in Ephesians, "Fathers, do not provoke your children to anger, but bring them up in the discipline and instruction of the Lord" (Eph. 6:4).

We must make a distinction between God's rules and our rules. Sometimes they do overlap, but sometimes they do not. There are often rules we have to make in our homes for the sake of order and peace. Put your dishes in the dishwasher when you are done. Take turns using the computer. Bedtime is at 9:00 p.m. My pastor explains to his children that there is a difference between the law of God and the rules they have in their house.[2] Such rules do not carry the same weight as God's law and cannot be equated with them. They are put in place because all households need rules to function. It is helpful to our children when we explain this difference.

Rules in Daily Life

Moses urged God's people to remind their children of who God is and His commands for them all throughout the day. That's because we are so forgetful. We have wayward and wandering hearts. We need frequent reminders. How can we teach and remind our children of God's rules for them and further, why they need such rules?

During devotional times, we can read God's word aloud to our children, teaching them who God is, what pleases Him, and why Jesus came to save us. We can help our children learn God's commands by having them memorize Bible verses and passages. When we teach them God's commands, we can ask questions such as: What does this command teach us about God and who He is? Can we perfectly keep this command? Why not? What did Jesus do for us in His perfect life? What do we do when we break one of God's commands, such as when we tell a lie or when we are unkind to our brother or sister?

Music is a powerful tool for learning and there are many verses set to song to aid in learning. Writing is another method for instruction. For children who are learning to write, they can practice writing by tracing Bible verses. Older children can write out entire passages. For as David wrote, "I have stored up your word in my heart, that I might not sin against you" (Ps. 119:11).

It's also helpful to post family rules in a place where everyone can see them. For young children who can't yet read, we can provide pictures or graphics to help them remember the rule. When they need a reminder, we can point to the rules and say, "Remember, in our house we always wash hands before dinner." Or, "In the Smith family, we show our love by helping one another."

In my own family, we've written out important rules in the form of an agreement. We've done this specifically in the area of screen time use. Both we as parents and our children developed the agreement together and then we all signed it. Having something in writing is helpful to consult and refer back to when either parent or child forgets the rules.

Limits are a good thing. We are all sinners and need to know what pleases God and what does not. Our Father gives us rules in His Word. These rules are for our good and in obeying them we glorify Him. As parents, we show our children who God is when we set limits for them. Whatever our rules, may they give God glory and may they point our children to their need for a Savior, Jesus Christ.

Questions for Discussion

1. What kinds of experiences did you have with rules growing up? How have these experiences shaped how you view rules and limits?

2. What rules do you have in your family? Why do we need rules and boundaries?

3. What is the purpose of the law for Christians? How does understanding the indicative and imperative help us understand God's instructions for us?

4. Read a section of Psalm 119. What does the psalmist love about God's law?

5. What are some examples of legalistic rules, those that add to God's law?

6. How might some rules exasperate our children? How can we know if a rule we set glorifies God or is for our own good and comfort?

7. How can you image God today in the limits you set for your children?

A Parent's Prayer

Father, I thank You for your law. It is perfect, holy, and just, as You are. Your law shows me Your goodness and what pleases You. Forgive me for my rebellious heart that seeks its own way. I pray You would give me a heart like the psalmist, a heart that loves Your law. When I read Your law and commands in the Bible, help me to see You and my need for Christ. Use me as a parent to show my children how much they need a Savior. Help me to set rules and limits that point to You.

In Jesus' name, amen.

5

GOD TEACHES
AND TRAINS US

Our family loves to hike together. We've traveled far and wide to explore mountain trails. When the kids were young, we started with easy mile-long trails in the north Georgia mountains. As they got older, we tried longer trails. We then added ones with steep inclines. The first time we attempted a four-mile hike with our boys, we were in Alaska visiting family. My husband and I were uncertain whether the trail would be too long and too arduous; it was the longest hike our sons had done yet. Not only that, it was a windy, brisk day. The path didn't have much in the way of elevation change, but it was long. The trail started in the woods, providing protection from the wind and cold. But as we got closer to the end, we left the cover of the trees and were open to the elements. It was freezing! Overall, my children did well on the hike. The youngest missed the final mile and turned around early with another family member. My husband and I were both excited at the success because it meant we could take them on longer trails. We've since hiked the redwood forests of Yosemite, the Cascades in Washington state, and the desert trails in Arches National Park.

When we go for a hike, some trails take us through difficult terrain. We find ourselves climbing uphill, crossing creeks and streams, and cautiously scooting across narrow ledges with steep drops just below our feet. We've even been on trails that were so steep, the park provided ropes to hold on to. The elevation change often leaves us breathless, and we stop for frequent water breaks. But then we get to the end of the trail and are rewarded with a stunning view. A waterfall. A deep canyon. An amazing arch. A panorama of snow-capped peaks.

Sometimes, I look back at the trail that brought us to our destination. I can see the long winding, switchback path that brought us to our reward. I can see how far we've come. While the hike was arduous and at times I wondered if we'd ever make it, it was worth it in the end. And I have the pictures to prove it!

This is true in my spiritual life. I often like to look back on the path I've traveled in my relationship with God. I marvel at His goodness and grace throughout the years. I remember who I once was and who I am now.

The Journey of Faith

I can see how all the paths I took led to me to where I am today. I can see how God brought me on short, easy trails at times and difficult trails at other times. I see places where I fell and needed help getting back up again. I see times where He provided necessary refreshment and rest, and times where I journeyed through dark and frightening paths, where the trail ahead was hidden, and

I had to focus on simply putting one foot in front of the other. But all along the way, I see God's faithfulness. I still have far to go, for my journey is not yet over. And though I've learned much in the journey, I know there is still much more to learn.

There's a wonderful book, an allegory that speaks to the Christian life as a journey, called *The Pilgrim's Progress*. It is the journey of a man named Christian who travels from the City of Destruction to the Celestial City. Along the way, he meets believers who encourage and help him, as well as unbelievers who distract and attempt to lead him astray. He has periods of rest and refreshment and times where he fights battles both within and without. He experiences doubt, hardship, and sorrow. He makes wrong turns and learns the consequences. In the end, he arrives at his destination. This centuries-long bestseller is helpful for all believers to understand how the Christian faith is a journey.

We are all on a journey—a faith journey. From the moment of salvation until we reach heaven's gates, God is teaching and preparing us for eternity with Him. He shows us the narrow path of life. He teaches us what it looks like to be a part of the family, of the rhythms and ways of His people. He teaches us what is right and good, with our elder brother Jesus as the perfect example. He cautions us against sin. He warns us of the consequences of wandering from Him. When we do stumble, He provides forgiveness and restoration through the blood of His Son. Throughout the journey, our Father is actively engaged in our training.

Likewise, parents are their children's first instructors. As we saw in the last chapter, Deuteronomy 6:4–8 teaches us that parents are to instruct their children about God—who He is and what He has done—all the time and everywhere: when we sit, when we walk, when we lie down, and when we rise. In this chapter, we are going to look at how God trains us in righteousness. He is making us into disciples. We'll then explore how we can image God to our children in how we disciple them—how we teach and train them in the path of life.

God's Training Ground

No matter how long you've been a Christian, you've been on a journey. No matter how far along you are on that journey, you can look back and see where God has brought you and what He has taught you along the way. Your Father has been with you each step of that journey, ensuring your training is thorough and complete.

Our Father's training ground is not found so much in a classroom, though there are things we learn about Him in classroom settings. His work in us doesn't center so much on improving all that we know so we can pass some sort of multiple-choice test on biblical trivia, though it does shape our knowledge of Him. It's also not focused so much on what people see on the outside, though our training does inevitably change what people see. Rather, the training ground is centered on our heart. God's training transforms the core and very essence of who we are, doing as He promised in Ezekiel: "And I will give you a new heart, and a new spirit I will put within you. And I will remove the heart of stone from your flesh and give you a heart of flesh. And I will put my Spirit within you, and cause you to walk in my statutes and be careful to obey my rules" (Ezek. 36:26–27).

In the New Testament, we read about the Pharisees. They were highly trained in the Old Testament Scriptures. They dedicated their lives to keeping the law, and then some. To ensure they followed the law, they created extra rules and guidelines, beyond what God had already given. To be sure, they knew a lot. But their knowledge remained just that. It didn't transform their lives. It didn't change their heart. Instead, their knowledge puffed them up. It made them think they could earn their righteousness before God. It made them think they were holy and everyone else was not. Then in stepped Jesus.

Throughout Jesus' ministry, He came up against the legalism and pride of the Pharisees. In Matthew 15, they spoke against Him because the disciples did not follow their hand washing rules. Jesus then recited Isaiah 29:13, saying, "This people honors me with their lips, but their heart is far from me; in vain do they worship me, teaching as doctrines the commandments of men" (Matt. 15:8–9). All their rules and attempts at holiness only drew them further from God rather than closer to Him. On the outside, it looked as though they were holy and righteous, but in their hearts, in the center of their being, they did not love Him. Their outward behavior might have conformed to a list of rules they created, but in their inner being, they remained cold and dead.

Jesus then went on to explain to the disciples that it is not what people take in that taints them, it's what is already within them. Not washing one's hands does not make one a sinner; rather, it's what arises out of the heart. He said,

> "But what comes out of the mouth proceeds from the heart, and this defiles a person. For out of the heart come evil thoughts, murder, adultery, sexual immorality, theft, false witness, slander. These are what defile a person. But to eat with unwashed hands does not defile anyone." (Matt. 15:18–20)

Our greatest problem—our sin—doesn't come from outside of us, but from inside. While we know this about ourselves, we must also remember this about our children. It's tempting at times to think that our child's greatest problem is something outside of themselves—friendships, school challenges, barriers to success—but their greatest problem is the same as ours: sin. Yet, through Christ, we have the solution to that problem: He cleansed us and made us new through His blood shed on the cross. And it's a solution we must share with our children!

After Jesus died, rose again, and ascended into heaven, the Father sent the Holy Spirit to live in the hearts of His people. In John 14, Jesus told His disciples what to expect from the Spirit: "But the Advocate, the Holy Spirit, whom the Father will send in my name, will teach you all things and will remind you of everything I have said to you" (v. 26 NIV). The Spirit has an important role in the training of our hearts. He teaches, trains, and leads us into righteousness. He reminds us what is true. He convicts us of sin, then helps strip away that sin so we can put on righteousness. He encourages our hearts and affirms our sonship. He prays to the Father on our behalf. He gives us gifts to use for God's glory. He produces fruit within us. All this work is a process; one we call sanctification.

Like the Pharisees, we might look at our growth in holiness (sanctification) as a work that we do; and it's true, there is some work on our part. We must yield to the Spirit's work within us. But our transformation is ultimately a work of the Spirit, and that work comes to us by God's grace. As Paul wrote in Titus 2:11–14:

> For the grace of God has appeared, bringing salvation for all people, training us to renounce ungodliness and worldly passions, and to live self-controlled, upright, and godly lives in the present age, waiting for our blessed hope, the appearing of the glory of our great God and Savior Jesus Christ, who gave himself for us to redeem us from all lawlessness and to purify for himself a people for his own possession who are zealous for good works.

We are not only saved by God's grace, but we are also trained by His grace. His grace trains us to put to death the sin within us and then trains us in how to live for Him. Paul reminds us this is why Christ died for us: to redeem us and then transform us into His people who live lives of godliness. What good news! God saves us by His grace, adopts us by His grace, and then transforms us by His grace. Grace upon grace upon grace.

> *We are not only saved by God's grace, but we are also trained by His grace. His grace trains us to put to death the sin within us and then trains us in how to live for Him.*

Methods in Training the Heart

What methods then does our Father use in training us to be like His Son? What does this training look like in our lives? Even more, what does it tell us about parenting our children? Much has been written on the process of sanctification, but here are few things to consider:

He Trains Us Where We Are

God meets us where we are. He doesn't stand off far ahead on the journey and call to us from afar. He comes near and trains us where we stand. He trains us right here and now, in our current circumstances. He meets us in our jobs, our homes, our relationships, our longings and desires, our sins and struggles, and in our sufferings. He uses every circumstance, big and small, to teach us about ourselves, our need for Him, and about who He is. Like a mom who leaves the playground bench to look her son in the eye and talk to him about the angry words he shouted at his sister, our

Father meets us in our own circumstances to instruct us in the way of righteousness.

Consider the way Jesus met the woman at the well in John 4. The Jews did not speak to Samaritans, much less to Samaritan women. Yet Jesus met this Samaritan woman at the well. Not only was she a Samaritan woman, she also led an outwardly sinful life. She had a series of husbands and the man she was with was not her husband (v. 18). Jesus spoke to her deepest need and desire and told her that He alone could fulfill it; only He could give her water that satisfies (vv. 13–14).

He Trains Us Over Time

The story of Christian in *The Pilgrim's Progress* takes place over the course of his life, from salvation to death. God trains us over the course of time—each moment of each day throughout our lives. While God looks at us as holy and righteous because of Christ's work for us, and while we've been set free from the power of sin over us, the presence of sin still remains within us. This is why our sanctification is a lifelong event. We battle against sin until we step into glory. In addition, God doesn't show us everything we need to learn at once; He reveals it gradually over time. Imagine if He showed us all that we needed to learn at once, how overwhelming that would be! Like a parent who gradually gives a growing child more and more responsibilities, first by folding towels, then by folding shirts and shorts, and then finally by teaching him to use the washing machine, God builds our instruction over time.

We see this in the life of Paul. Early in his Christian life, he described himself as the least of the disciples (1 Cor. 15:9). He had persecuted the church and did not feel worthy of being a disciple. Later in his life, after he grew more in his faith and saw more of the depths of his sin, he described himself as the worst of all sinners (1

Tim. 1:15 NIV). The closer he got to God, the more he realized how holy God is, and how unholy he was in contrast. He didn't become more of a sinner as he got older; he just increasingly saw who he really was and how much he needed the grace of God in his life.

His Training Isn't Always Linear

Though we are headed forward to an end goal, eternity with God forever, our training isn't always linear. In the allegory of *The Pilgrim's Progress*, we see Christian make progress in his journey, and other times he gets stuck. Or he is tempted and wanders off the path. Or he gets wounded in battle. So too with us. We don't necessarily learn a lesson once and then move on from that lesson. Sometimes, lessons are repeated. We may seem to move on from a lesson and then later have to return and learn it again. Sometimes, we practice one same lesson our entire lives. I often remind myself of this truth when I find myself repeating the same lesson to my child. If I have to learn and re-learn lessons, I shouldn't be surprised that my children have to as well.

We see Peter learning similar lessons in the gospels. He was impulsive and frequently said the wrong thing at the wrong time. Though he was the first of the disciples to profess who Christ was (Matt. 16:16), he also spoke out against Jesus' teaching that He would suffer and die (Matt. 16:22). He struggled with and gave in to his fears, both when Jesus was arrested and three times before the rooster crowed (Matt. 26:75), and also when he feared what the Judaizers thought of him (Gal. 2:11–14). But the Lord worked in Peter and he ultimately learned and grew from those experiences. He later wrote these words:

> In this you rejoice, though now for a little while, if necessary, you have been grieved by various trials, so that the tested

genuineness of your faith—more precious than gold that perishes though it is tested by fire—may be found to result in praise and glory and honor at the revelation of Jesus Christ. (1 Peter 1:6–7)

Peter became the rock Christ called him to be. So too with us. We may have stops and starts, we may stumble time and again, but God finishes the work He begins in us.

He Trains Us Differently

In *The Pilgrim's Progress*, Christian meets a friend named Faithful who joins him in his journey for a while until he loses his life in the city of Vanity. While their journeys overlapped for a time, Faithful's journey was different than Christian's. This is true for us as believers; no two Christians have the same story. Some of us were born into Christian homes and learned who God is at an early age. Others were saved later in life. We also have different stories in how God trains and sanctifies us. Some of us have different lessons to learn than others. We all have different sins and temptations. We all experience different types of suffering and hardships.

Consider the apostles. Paul was uniquely called while on the way to Damascus to arrest Christians. Peter struggled with the fear of man. Thomas needed to touch Jesus' wounds before he believed Christ had risen. Some of the apostles learned beforehand how they would suffer and die for Christ (John 21:19; Acts 9:16). Others did not. The apostle John was not a martyr but spent time marooned on an island. God teaches and trains His children in different ways according to their needs and His will for their lives. Whatever those ways are, they are for our good (Rom. 8:28).

He Trains Us Through His Word

In John 17:17, Jesus prayed, "Sanctify them in the truth; your word is truth." The Bible is the primary tool the Spirit uses to change us. Paul told Timothy that God's word is "breathed out by God and profitable for teaching, for reproof, for correction, and for training in righteousness" (2 Tim. 3:16). While other books we read may impact our lives in some way, only the Word of God is alive. Only God's Word can see into the heart, "For the word of God is living and active, sharper than any two-edged sword, piercing to the division of soul and of spirit, of joints and of marrow, and discerning the thoughts and intentions of the heart" (Heb. 4:12). As we read, study, and meditate on God's Word, it convicts us of sin, points us to the gospel, teaches us about who God is, reveals to us the path of life, and prepares us for eternity. The Word of God is our very life (Deut. 32:47).

He Trains Us Through Life Experiences

Our training isn't lived out in the confines of a lab; rather, it takes place in our daily life. As we face daily challenges, both big and small, we have opportunities to learn and grow in our faith. At the traffic light when we are running late to work, we might learn to put to death our anger or to trust in God's sovereignty over our time. When suffering and trial enter our lives, we learn lessons then as well—lessons of trust, perseverance, and of God's strength in our weakness. We learn not to depend on ourselves, but on the grace of God. When we respond to our children with impatience and harsh words, we learn then too. We learn more of our need for Christ and His forgiveness of sins. Sometimes we learn lessons when our idols are challenged in some way, such as when our children don't succeed at something in the way we expect. We learn then that God alone is our life and hope, and that no counterfeit god or idol can satisfy. All our life experiences are divinely placed opportunities for us to learn and grow in holiness.

He Trains Us Alongside Others

Our Father doesn't train us in isolation; He trains us in the context of community—the church. He uses our brothers and sisters in Christ to encourage, equip, and exhort us forward in the faith. They remind us who we are and of our identity as God's own child. They point us to the gospel and urge us to keep our eyes fixed on our elder brother, Jesus Christ, who paid for our sins. They disciple us in the faith, teaching us what they have learned from God and His Word. They mourn with us, rejoice with us, and share with us all they have. At times, they point out when we've wandered off the narrow path and help us find our way back. And, as Trillia Newbell noted, "Relationships in the church can be a means by which God draws us to himself."[1] The honest and vulnerable relationships we have with others in the church can help us learn to be honest and vulnerable with our Father. Learning to depend on our brothers and sisters as they walk alongside us in this journey can show us how to grow in greater dependence on our Father.

In the same way too, we parent our children in the context of a community, in a family. Like the body of Christ, we also encourage, disciple, and exhort our children to know the Lord and grow in their faith. And the relationship we have with our children help them learn how to relate to their Father in heaven.

As we can see, our Father is intentional in training us in the way of righteousness. He uses a variety of means and circumstances. He trains us where we are and with the exact lesson we need. Take some time to consider all the ways God teaches you who He is and what He has done. How might your Father's training impact the training or discipleship of your children?

Training Our Children

As parents, it is a privilege to introduce our children to their Father in heaven. It's not only a privilege, but also an important responsibility, and one we can't take lightly. In Psalm 78, the psalmist writes about a parent's duty to pass on the truths of God to the next generation:

> We will not hide them from their children, but tell to the coming generation the glorious deeds of the LORD, and his might, and the wonders that he has done. He established a testimony in Jacob and appointed a law in Israel, which he commanded our fathers to teach to their children, that the next generation might know them, the children yet unborn, and arise and tell them to their children, so that they should set their hope in God and not forget the works of God, but keep his commandments. (vv. 4–7)

This psalm reminds us that we have a God-given responsibility to teach and train our children to know God—who He is and what He has done for us in Christ. We are their primary teachers. Though they will have other people in their life who mentor and disciple them in God's word—Sunday school teachers, youth leaders, grandparents, and more—we have the primary role to disciple our children. This does not mean we are responsible for their salvation; that is a free gift of God (Eph. 2:8). Just as God uses our prayers to carry out His will—He doesn't need to, but chooses to—so too God chooses to use parents as a means by which He works in the hearts of our children to draw them to Himself. We need to be intentional in teaching and training our children in the faith. We do so, trusting not in our efforts but in the Lord and His work in their lives.

When we consider the ways in which God trains us, it informs the ways we train our children. Of course, our training is limited by our humanity and our sin, and we are not training our children to sanctify them (that is the Spirit's work). Our training serves to point our children to God. Let's consider a few ways we can image God in that training.

Imaging God in Our Training

Each of my children is an athlete. Since preschool, they've participated in both team and individual sports. Over the years, they've had coaches who vary in terms of temperament, coaching style, and how they respond to the players. Some were more like drill sergeants, yelling at and even belittling team members who didn't measure up. Others took different tactics, including providing training in areas of weakness, verbally encouraging the players, and noticing effort and improvement. It goes without saying that my sons responded positively to certain coaches and less so to others. In fact, one coach completely turned my children off to a sport altogether! Indeed, a good coach makes a significant impact in a player's performance.

As parents, we are training our children, not in a sport, but to know God. The apostle Paul likened the journey of faith to that of a race (1 Cor. 9:24; 2 Tim. 4:7). We want to train our children to understand the race of faith. We want to equip and prepare them to live for God and His glory. Like coaches, we have a training ground, a place where we focus our training. Also like a coach, we utilize specific tools to help our children grow in their knowledge of God. And as we train, we'll start where our children currently are, increasing the training as they mature.

In keeping with our topic, how can we train our children as the Father trains us?

Training the Heart

Our Father's training is focused on the heart. This is true for us in our parenting; we need to teach to their heart. Merely focusing on outward conformity, trying to control all the influences in their life, and closely monitoring everything they do will not reach the heart. Though I have to admit this is tempting. Sometimes, I just want my children to conform. I want to teach them what is right and then sit back and watch as they immediately comply. Yet it just doesn't work that way, does it? The more I consider the ways God trains me, the more I realize that my own children need to see the true state of their condition as sinners and of their need for Jesus.

When our children struggle with sin, we can view it not as an inconvenient interruption, nor as a reason to be embarrassed in front of our friends, but as an opportunity to remind them why they sin: because all people sin. We also can remind them that our sin keeps us from relationship with God, but because of Jesus, we can be forgiven. Together, we can pray to God about that sin, asking for His help and forgiveness. Going through this process gets to the heart.

If we spent the bulk of our parenting focused on outward conformity to rules and not on helping our children recognize they are sinners in need of a Savior, they will grow to think they are capable of being good. They will strive to "be good" on the outside, but not know their Savior on the inside. This means we need to keep the gospel front and center in all our teaching, pointing them to their need for Christ and His great love for them poured out at the cross. As Paul Tripp wrote, "Parenting is about being used of God to bring your children to that wholesome and heart-changing place of personal hopelessness. This is not a process of condemnation, but of patient and loving rescue."[2] As we teach our children who God is and what He has done, as we teach them the way of righteousness, we remind them over and over that they cannot be righteous on their own; they need a Savior.

> *If we spent the bulk of our parenting focused on outward conformity to rules and not on helping our children recognize they are sinners in need of a Savior, they will grow to think they are capable of being good.*

Training in God's Word

God's Word is the source for our training. Just as it is sufficient for the Spirit's work in our hearts, it is sufficient for training our children. We want to read it to our children and teach them what it says. As they mature, we teach them how to read and study it for themselves. As my children have grown, I've enjoyed teaching them tools for studying the Bible on their own. We also help them learn the grand meta-story of the Bible: the story of creation, fall, redemption, and restoration. We help them understand how God created them in His image, how sin entered the world, and what God did about it by sending His Son to die for sin.

Many times, I've used this big story to answer questions my children have about suffering, cultural issues, and their own sin struggles. Our children also need to learn that God is a God of grace and how everything He does is an act of grace. They need to learn what sin is and how to repent of it and receive forgiveness. We also teach them about prayer and how to tell God about their hurts, sorrows, and fears. As our children grow and mature, they'll need to develop a biblical worldview and how to look at all things through the lens of Scripture. In addition, they need to learn what the Bible teaches about the nature of God, His characteristics, His names, His works, and His ways. When you stop and consider it, there is so much to teach them!

When I get overwhelmed thinking about all I want my children to understand about the Lord, I remind myself that my teaching takes place over the course of their childhood, not all at once. I also remember that the Lord uses other people in my children's lives to teach and reinforce the truths they learn at home: grandparents, pastors, Sunday school teachers, etc. And, as is true in my own life, my children will continue to learn and grow after leaving home. For all believers, spiritual training continues throughout our lives. So rather than fear that I've not done enough, I do my best and pray that the Lord is gracious and uses it in my children's lives.

Our teaching will be both organized and spontaneous. At times, we will want to map out what they need to learn, just as a teacher might develop her lesson plans for the year. We might decide to focus on the incarnation during the month of December, teaching our children why Jesus came to earth as a baby. In our family, we often utilized an Advent devotional and made ornaments for each day of the season. Another time, we might teach them the attributes of God, so they understand who He is. One of my favorite studies with my own children was when we studied the names of God. I didn't realize there were so many!

We want to develop consistent times where we teach them from God's Word, but there are also times when we simply want to take advantage of natural teaching moments. When we are at the park and our young child is fascinated by a particular animal or plant, we can talk about the wonder of our Creator God. When our child asks questions from his seat in the back of the car while we drive, we can steer the conversation to truths about God. I can't count the number of times one of my kids asked, "Why did God . . .?" while I drove down the road. When we watch a movie with our teen, we can use the topics in the movie to generate discussions that speak to biblical truths. As the English poet John Milton wrote, "The end of learning is to repair the ruin of our first parents by regaining to know God aright, and out of that knowledge to love him, to imitate him, to be like him."[3]

Training Where They Are

When my children were younger, they wanted to help me prepare dinner. I was chopping up vegetables and I think what they really wanted to do was use the knife! But they were too young and untrained to use a knife, so we started with learning how to measure ingredients. They learned cooking at their level and over time, they increased in their learning. Today, they can cook a meal all on their own. God does the same with us. Over the years in my own faith, God has taught me things in increments, as I was ready to learn them. I would surely have been overwhelmed had He shown me my sin all at once!

Just as God trains us where we are, we too teach and train our children where they are. We teach them where they are developmentally—physically, socially, emotionally, educationally, and spiritually. We wouldn't teach a two-year-old the same way we would instruct a twelve-year-old. We would teach them about God in ways that meet their developmental needs. When they are young, it helps to keep our training brief and to the point. We might focus on using hands-on activities, stories, and music in our instruction. My children loved learning Bible verses through song. They also enjoyed doing craft projects and activities that helped them remember something they learned. One time, we made cardboard swords and shields when learning about Paul's teaching on the armor of God in Ephesians 6. As you can imagine, it was a big hit with my sons! It is also helpful to use objects and illustrations they can relate to. I've often used illustrations directly from my children's favorite television shows or the books they read and compared them to spiritual truths.

As they grow, we add to our instruction. We read longer passages of Scripture aloud and talk about what we read, helping them think through how the Bible intersects with their life at school and with their friendships. We talk more about the culture around them and how the gospel speaks to contemporary circumstances. These days, my teens have a lot of questions about our world and how they ought to respond to what they see and hear. I find myself framing my responses through the lens of the Bible's grand story, reminding my children how things are supposed to be, what happened to make things the way they are, the only solution to our problem, and how God will one day make all things new.

We know their learning will change as they grow and mature (we'll look at this more in a later chapter). It will also change as they mature spiritually and make a profession of their faith. Our training is gradual and builds upon itself throughout their formative years. We may start singing Bible verses to our little ones and then in their preschool years graduate to helping them memorize a Bible verse. As they mature, they will learn longer passages of Scripture. One year, we memorized a few chapters in the book of James together. My kids seemed to master it easily; I can't say the same for myself! When our children are little, we may focus on teaching them how much God loves them. We may talk about loving and glorifying God by speaking kind words to others, serving family members, and sharing with their friends. As they grow, we teach them the way of wisdom in the Proverbs and how Jesus is wisdom incarnate. We talk about how the gospel shapes our actions toward others. Just as our Father teaches us more and more as we mature in our faith, we build our instruction over the years with our children.

As we teach our children, we don't expect them to master what we've taught them the first time, and we know they will need to repeat lessons. We also know our children won't learn everything they need to learn while under our roof. Consider all the lessons God has taught you in adulthood! There is much God will continue to teach our children throughout their life. We want to help them build a foundation that will carry them through into adulthood—biblical truths they can lean on and cling to in whatever circumstances they encounter in their journey of faith.

It can be overwhelming to think of all the truths we want to teach our children about God. We must remember that all our teaching is dependent on the Spirit and His work in us and in our children. So we teach while on our knees in prayer. We pray that the Lord uses our efforts. We pray that He nurtures the seeds we plant and then brings in a rich harvest in our children's lives. We must rest on the grace of God, the very same grace we point our children to.

Questions for Discussion

1. What has the Father taught you so far in your faith journey?

2. How have you seen His grace for you in that training?

3. Why is it important that we teach and train to our child's heart?

4. Read Mark 4. How did Jesus teach the disciples? What does this show you about how you can teach your children who God is and what He has done for them?

5. Our Father is gracious in how He meets us where we are and trains us according to what we are ready for. In what ways can you image this to your children?

6. What role should God's Word have in our training? What are some practical ways you can use the Bible in your teaching?

7. How can you image God today in the way you train your children in righteousness?

A Parent's Prayer

Father in heaven, when I look back to where I once was and where I am now, I am struck anew at Your love and grace for me. I thank You for your Spirit who never ceases His work within me. Help me as I seek to point my children to who You are and all You have done for them in Christ. Help me to model all that I teach. I pray the Spirit would give them a new heart so that they would know You. I pray You would change and transform them to be like Christ.

In Jesus' name, amen.

6

GOD DISCIPLINES US

Have you ever had this experience? You need a few things from the grocery store in order to make dinner so you gather up the kids and head to the store. You want to just run in and out. No detours. No special stops. Just grab those few items and return home. No big deal, right?

Except that it's the time of day where all kids seem to lose all self-control, and your kids are no exception. The whining starts the minute you walk into the store. They fight over who gets to sit in the cart and who gets to walk. You get it sorted out and start to head to the meat section, when one child reminds you that you *always* stop at the bakery first for the free cookie. Detour #1. You go as quickly as you can, grab your pound of ground round, and scoot over to pasta aisle. There, in front of the spaghetti and fettuccini, one child insists she has to use the bathroom . . . right now! Detour #2. You finally head to the dairy section for the mozzarella when another fight breaks out, and while you are dealing with the fight, one child breaks free from your handhold and runs over to the ice cream section. Because, you know, Detour #3.

You get in line to pay and one child begs for something from the candy placed conveniently right at his eye level. You remind him dinner is coming up and he just had a cookie. He falls to the ground and starts crying. People are staring at you with what you perceive are looks of judgment. You can imagine what they are thinking. Your face starts to turn red. All you wanted was a few items to make dinner and instead, you got a combination of WWIII and a three-ring circus. How do you wrangle the masses? How do you all get out of the store in one piece? And how do you then respond to the chaos?

As I wrote at the start of this book, we all have parenting questions, specifically how-to parenting questions. Most of my parenting questions have centered around discipline. From the moment my crawling baby started exploring and getting into things he shouldn't, I wanted to know the best ways to discipline him. Those questions have not stopped since we entered the teenage years. Somehow, it seems discipline has become more difficult and more complicated. When my husband and I get together with other parents of teenagers, we all look back to the days when we could simply pick up our child and move him away from what we didn't want him to touch or we could take a toy away from squabbling siblings. These days, the troubles teenagers face have far greater consequences; their sins come at a greater cost to themselves and to others, making questions of discipline take on greater significance.

While it can be easy to romanticize or minimize the struggles of the past, I remember well the multitude of questions that swirled around my mind when my boys were younger. Questions like: What is the right form of discipline? How do I know when/what/how discipline is called for in a situation? How do I keep my child from having a tantrum at the check-out lane of the grocery store? How do I get my child to take his nap? How do I deal with their talking back? And on and on.

If I ever voiced those questions in the hearing of anyone nearby, there was always a ready opinion waiting. And I heard many! It's amazing how many different voices want to speak into the topic of discipline. While I did learn a few things from those who had walked the parenting journey before me, I think the best parenting wisdom comes from our Father Himself.

As my children moved on from the little years and into the school-age years, I found myself thinking more and more about how God has parented and continues to parent me. Whenever I would grow frustrated with a child's rebellious heart, the Spirit would gently prompt my memory to recall my own rebellious heart. I'd remember my own childhood, my own sin, and the ways the Lord worked in my life. Thinking through the Lord's discipline in my life helps frame the way I think about the discipline of my own children.

This chapter is about discipline, but not so much on the how-to of discipline. Rather, we are going to look at our Father's discipline of us and then what we learn from it so that it might shape our own discipline and how we image the Father to our children.

Our Father's Discipline

The book of Hebrews was written to Jewish Christians of the dispersion. They were facing persecution for their faith. Some had lost jobs; others had lost status in the community. They were kicked out of the synagogue, the place of belonging and community. Martyrdom seemed likely in their future. These believers were struggling. Some were tempted to forsake gathering for worship. They were afraid and filled with doubts. The author to these believers wrote a letter (more like a sermon series) encouraging them in their faith with the truth of how Jesus is greater than everything, including Moses, the angels, and the temple sacrifices.

Following the famous "Hall of Fame" chapter where the saints of old are listed is chapter 12. Here the author begins by encouraging his readers to keep their eyes fixed on Christ who suffered and died for them, for He is both the founder and perfecter of their faith (v. 2). The writer of Hebrews points out that they have not endured suffering to the extent their Savior did. He encourages them not to give up but to persevere. He then quotes from the book of Proverbs to explain the suffering that Christians experience.

And have you forgotten the exhortation that addresses you as sons? "My son, do not regard lightly the discipline of the Lord, nor be weary when reproved by him. For the Lord disciplines the one he loves, and chastises every son whom he receives." It is for discipline that you have to endure. God is treating you as sons. For what son is there whom his father does not discipline? If you are left without discipline, in which all have participated, then you are illegitimate children and not sons. Besides this, we have had earthly fathers who disciplined us and we respected them. Shall we not much more be subject to the Father of spirits and live? For they disciplined us for a short time as it seemed best to them, but he disciplines us for our good, that we may share his holiness. For the moment all discipline seems painful rather than pleasant, but later it yields the peaceful fruit of righteousness to those who have been trained by it. (Heb. 12:5–11)

This is a rich passage, showing us how God parents us and, specifically, how He disciplines us. Let's dig into it.

Discipline vs. Punishment

The word "discipline" used in Hebrews 12 is *paideia*. It means "the rearing of a child, training, discipline."[1] It is used to refer to teaching and instruction, as well as chastisement and correction for wrongdoing. This same word is also found in 2 Timothy 3:16–17, where Paul describes the Word of God as an instrument for our discipline: "All Scripture is breathed out by God and profitable for teaching, for reproof, for correction, and for training in righteousness, that the man of God may be complete, equipped for every good work." Our Father uses discipline to train us in the way of righteousness, to make us holy. Sometimes it is instructional in nature; other times it is correcting. In the context of this Hebrews 12 passage, God used the suffering these believers experienced for their training; it was used as discipline.

All chastisement or correction from our Father is intended for our training in righteousness.

Discipline is not the same thing as punishment. Have you ever encountered some kind of hardship or suffering in your life and thought, *God is angry with me, that's why this happened. I didn't pray enough. I didn't believe enough. I didn't trust enough.* I have thought such things, as though God was exacting retribution for my wrongdoing. Yet this passage teaches that while God does discipline us, He does not punish us. Jesus bore our punishment at the cross when God poured out

His wrath upon Him (Isa. 53:5). God has no more wrath for us. All chastisement or correction from our Father is intended for our training in righteousness. Therefore, we are not to grow weary from it. Instead, we are to take it seriously and learn from it. As Nancy Guthrie wrote, "Our suffering is not punishment sent from God, but as we trust God in the midst of it, he can use it as a tool for discipline . . . . If we give in to grumbling and complaining about the hardships and difficulties in our lives, we will miss out on what there is to learn from them."[2]

Training as Sons

This passage also points to our sonship. God disciplines us because we are His children. And He does so out of love. He desires that we be like His Son, Jesus, and He will do what it takes to develop the character of Christ in us. As Charles Spurgeon noted:

> When he afflicts his child, chastisement is applied in love, his strokes are, all of them, put there by the hand of love. . . . God doth not afflict willingly, nor grieve us for nought, but out of love and affection, because he perceives that if he leaves us unchastised, we shall bring upon ourselves misery ten thousand-fold greater than we shall suffer by his slight rebukes, and the gentle blows of his hand.[3]

Discipline is inherent to the duty of parents. Like our earthly father, our heavenly Father disciplines us to teach us. If He did not do so, then it would prove we are not His children. In this passage, the author may be alluding to the Roman tradition where illegitimate sons of Roman nobles were provided for financially but left undisciplined, whereas legitimate children were trained and prepared to inherit the father's estate.[4] When our Father disciplines us, it proves we belong to Him; it is evidence of our sonship.

Perfect Discipline

As the writer of Hebrews 12 observes, we've all experienced discipline from our earthly fathers. Likely, there were times when we thought their discipline was excessive or unfair. As we matured into adulthood, we may have looked back on the discipline we experienced and realized the discipline was necessary after all. For those who experienced abuse at the hands of their earthly fathers, this passage reminds us that we have a perfect Father in heaven whose discipline is always right and good. The author to the Hebrews uses an argument from lesser (earthly fathers) to greater (our heavenly Father). Our earthly fathers disciplined us as seemed right at the time. They did their best in their fallen humanity to train us. Yet our Father in heaven is perfect and only does what is right. His discipline is *always* necessary, timely, and for our ultimate good.

Discipline That Yields Righteousness

Our Father's discipline has an eternal goal in mind. Its purpose isn't just to get us to conform outwardly to rules; it is to change and transform us from the inside out. Our Father's discipline serves to make us more like Christ, "that we may share his holiness" (Heb. 12:10). For as James wrote, "Count it all joy, my brothers, when you meet trials of various kinds, for you know that the testing of your faith produces steadfastness. And let steadfastness have its full effect, that you may be perfect and complete, lacking in nothing" (James 1:2–4). The challenges, trials, and sufferings we face in this life shape our hearts and minds to image Christ. This is why James could tell us to "count it all joy," because we know the sorrow is temporary. What is lasting is our completeness, our holiness. When we enter into glory, we will be shed once and for all of all our sin and stand perfect before our Father in heaven.

All for Our Good

For many believers, Romans 8:28 is a passage they cling to in times of suffering and trial: "And we know that for those who love God all things work together for good, for those who are called according to his purpose." It's a passage that reminds us that God can turn any heartache and sorrow into our ultimate good. But what is that ultimate good? The next verse tells us, "For those whom he foreknew he also predestined to be conformed to the image of his Son, in order that he might be the firstborn among many brothers" (v. 29). Our Father uses all the circumstances in our lives to conform us into the image of His Son.

It's important that we understand just what the suffering is that we experience.[5] In part, some of our suffering comes simply from living in a fallen and broken world. This world is not as it should be. When our first parents sinned, it brought death and decay to all things. It's why we get sick. It's why storms and fires and other natural disasters wreak havoc in our world. Second, we also experience suffering as a natural result or consequence of our sinful choices or the sin of others. "The iniquities of the wicked ensnare him, and he is held fast in the cords of his sin" (Prov. 5:22). "Whoever sows injustice will reap calamity, and the rod of his fury will fail" (Prov. 22:8). God allows us to experience the natural results of our sin.

Sometimes we experience the consequences of another's sin, as when a spouse gambles away a family's savings or when a person runs a red light and totals our car. And a third form of suffering comes to us from Satan himself. This was Job's experience. Satan came to God and asked if he could cause Job to suffer, for he wanted Job to curse God in response (see Job 2). God is not the cause of our sin or that of anyone else, but He uses all these forms of suffering to train us in righteousness. As a surgeon uses a knife, God uses suffering with precision and care to bring about our good—to make us holy.

Imaging God in Our Discipline

This chapter closely relates to the last one. You might consider it part two of the discussion on training our children. While the previous chapter focused on teaching and training our children to know who God is, this chapter's focus is on training our children when they sin. The principles we previously looked at carry over into this one. For example, as we consider the ways we teach and train our children through discipline, we must also consider where our children are developmentally. We wouldn't discipline a two-year-old the same way we would a twelve-year-old. We also wouldn't have the same expectations for a preschooler as we would a high schooler. The younger a child, the more we can expect to have to teach and reteach, all the while reminding ourselves how often the Lord teaches us the same lessons over and over. In addition, the importance of God's Word holds true not only for teaching our children about God, but also for their correction. For as we'll soon see, the truths of the gospel are necessary in discipline.

As we consider the ways our Father trains us through discipline, there are ways in which the training of our children will differ from our own training. Again, we are not the Holy Spirit. We are not tasked with transforming our children into the image of Christ. However, we *are* to point our children to their need for a Savior. We are to show them the way of life. When they stray from the narrow path, we steer them back to it. This happens not only during times of Bible reading or family worship, but also as we discipline or correct them for wrongdoing.

This chapter isn't intended to discuss the particular forms of discipline we might use—there are plenty of books out there that speak to this. Instead, I want to focus on what we learn from our Father's discipline and how it can shape the ways we discipline our children. And more, how we show our children who God is through our discipline.

The Need for Discipline

Have you ever met an undisciplined child? Perhaps you were at a gathering with other parents and their children and one child seemed to do whatever he wanted without any intervention by his parents. They never told him to stop when he did something unsafe. They never chastised him when he was unkind to other children. It was apparent he ruled the family, rather than his parents being the authority figures. He lacked training.

This passage in Hebrews 12 makes it clear that children are to be disciplined. The author quotes from Proverbs 3, where Solomon exhorts his son to trust in the Lord with all his heart, to fear the Lord, and to honor Him. He wants his son to know that God's discipline is a good thing and not to despise it. Elsewhere in Proverbs we read, "He dies for lack of discipline, and because of his great folly he is led astray" (Prov. 5:23); and, "Discipline your son, for there is hope; do not set your heart on putting him to death" (Prov. 19:18). Under Jewish law, a rebellious son (one who was of age to be held accountable for his sin) could be put to death for disobedience (see Deut. 21:18–21). This passage exhorts parents to discipline and train children to keep them from the deadly consequences for their sin.

While our own children are not held to the Mosaic Law as the original readers of Proverbs were, we know that a child left undisciplined will continue down a destructive path. We also know that parents are responsible for teaching and training their children to stay on the path of life. The author of Proverbs teaches his son the way of wisdom and contrasts that with the way of folly (see Prov. 4 and following). Ultimately, wisdom is a person, Jesus Christ. As parents, we take every opportunity to teach our children their need for a Savior, including when we correct them for sin. As the Hebrews 12 passage implies, discipline is something a loving parent does. If we don't discipline, then we are not loving our children.

Our children are sinners; they were born that way. As the psalmist wrote, "Behold, I was brought forth in iniquity, and in sin did my mother conceive me" (Ps. 51:5). Because our children are sinners, they *will* sin. We should not be surprised by this. We should not be shocked if our son or daughter pushes another kid down to grab a toy. We should not be caught off guard if our daughter lies to avoid trouble. We should not be naïve about the temptations our children face and give in to. Because they are sinners, they need training. They need to know what is right and what is wrong. They need to know there are consequences for wrongdoing, and they need us to give them those consequences. They need to be corrected and shown the way of wisdom, the way that leads to Christ. They need to know of God's grace for them through Christ's sacrifice for sin at the cross. They need discipline.

The Purpose of Discipline

We see from our Father's discipline that the purpose of His discipline is not punitive; rather, it is for training in righteousness. The focus of our discipline is training as well; however, we can't change or control our children, only the Holy Spirit can. Our job is to help our children learn from what they've done wrong and help them see their sin and their need for a Savior. We want them to repent of their sin and seek forgiveness from God. We want to help them learn to appropriate the gospel to their sin, to acknowledge that they cannot save themselves, and that they need God's grace poured out for them in Christ.

This means our discipline is not about us and expressing our anger. It is not about getting even with our child. The purpose of discipline is not to satisfy our own emotions. It's also not an occasion to belittle or respond in sarcasm. Discipline is not about throwing our arms up in the air and asking in anger, "What's wrong with you?" Discipline is not abusive. Rather, our discipline is about training and correction. It is showing them what they have done wrong, why it is wrong, and helping them learn to repent. It is teaching them what to do next time. It is providing consequences that help them in the learning.

Sometimes, as the Father does with us, we allow natural consequences to teach our children. When my oldest was in kindergarten, he attended a school that had a rule that if a child forgot his lunch, his parent was not allowed to bring it to the school. The school would provide him a basic sandwich for lunch. They wanted children to learn to take responsibility for themselves and not rely on their parents to protect them from the consequences of their actions. In a similar way, when we allow our children to experience the consequences of their choices—not calling the teacher to intervene when our child doesn't get an A because she chose not to study for the test—they have an opportunity to learn. We can then process with them the natural consequence: why it happened, what they can learn from it, how they might handle the situation next time.

Other times we will use different means to train our children. Sometimes it may simply be saying no to something we know is not good for our child. How often do we say no to an extra piece of candy? We do so because we know the harmful effects of sugar on teeth. There are times when we need to say no to harmful things and doing so is a loving thing. Discipline can also look like a conversation where we sit down with our children and correct them for wrongdoing, discussing why a behavior is sinful and what is expected next time. We might even help them practice doing or saying the right thing—role-playing if you will. Often when my children were young I had them practice out loud how to respond to each other during a conflict.

Sometimes discipline looks like following through on a previously stated consequence for breaking a rule. We have specific guidelines in our house about technology use and I recently took away phone privileges for a day to be consistent with those rules and consequences. Other times, discipline is providing a consequence that provides short-term discomfort in the hopes it will teach a long-term lesson. There are even times when discipline can be humorous. I remember an occasion when my children were younger, and they spent the entire day bickering with each other. I took one of my husband's T-shirts and put it over both of them. I then handed them a laundry basket and instructed them to get the clothes out of the dryer and separate them into piles. They giggled and laughed the entire time. I then explained to them the importance of their unity as brothers. Whatever the discipline, its purpose is training.

As someone who used to teach parenting skills, I often heard this complaint from parents who tried to implement a specific type of disciplinary action: "It didn't work." They expected that the discipline they were taught to use would "work." And by "work" they meant that they expected the discipline to somehow make their child stop misbehaving. They wanted the behavior to go away. Yet, the Bible is clear that we are fallen in sin. Our children are fallen in sin. They will continue to sin and continue to need correction and training. Martin Luther wrote in his Ninety-five Theses that the life of the Christian is one of repentance.[6] Our discipline will not make our children stop sinning; rather, it serves to help them see their sin, learn to repent, and seek forgiveness through Christ.

The Focus of Discipline

The focus of our discipline is on the heart. While we could train our children for outward conformity, and they might appear well-behaved to people around them, if their heart is rebellious, that training won't last. It won't impact their spiritual condition. Our children are spiritual descendants of Adam and Eve; they are born with a heart that naturally wants its own way. They want to rule their own lives. They don't want mom or dad telling them what to do, where to go, what to eat, when to sleep. They want to be kings and queens of their own kingdoms. Paul Tripp explains this inherently deluded way of thinking: "Every child tends to think that being told what to do is a negative thing. Every child wants to write his own moral rules and follow his own life plan. The delusion of the right to self-rule is one of the sad results of sin in the hearts of all of our children."[7] But we understand this desire for self-rule, don't we? For we are born into the same sinful condition as our children. We know the direction of their hearts because ours have the same bent—until the grace of God gripped our hearts and made us new.

That's why our job as image-bearing parents is so important. God gave us authority over our children to teach them and show them and point them to their ultimate authority: God Himself. This means we direct our discipline to our children's wayward hearts, which innately desire to go their own way. When we discipline, we point out not only their disobedience, we reveal to them the source of it. We can then teach them they need Someone outside themselves to rescue them. They need Jesus' rescuing and saving grace. Yes, we provide consequences for sinful actions. But while doing so, we remind them over and over of the gospel.

We also share with our children how the gospel has impacted and changed our own hearts. We need to make it clear that we are sinners too and that we need Jesus' rescuing grace. One way to do this is with our own sin. When we sin against our children, we have an opportunity to model for them what repentance looks like. With my own children, I know it speaks volumes when my husband and I are quick to apologize for our actions.

Further, we have an opportunity to point our children to the heart of the Father in the way we respond to their sin—not in anger, but in compassionate understanding, for we too are prone to sin; not out of fear of what others think of us, but out of love for the hearts of our children; not in a desire to control, but in trust of the One who brings dead hearts to life. For as we respond to our children out of the abundant grace we've received, they will see Him through us.

Discipline That Seems Best

As parents, we want to get everything right. That's why we ask all the how-to questions. We want to raise our children well and parent in a way that glorifies God. We don't want to fail. Above all, we want our children to come to a saving faith in Jesus Christ. Hebrews 12:10 gently reminds us that our parenting is limited by our humanity: "They disciplined us for a short time as it seemed best to them." We *will* make mistakes in our parenting. We are restricted by the limited information we have about a situation. Our own sin creates a barrier in our parenting. We can only do our best and our best will never be perfect. That's why we have to remember that God will parent our children perfectly. He will be everything we cannot be. He will take our stumbling and imperfect efforts and use them in His ongoing work in our children's hearts. God only calls us to teach and train our children; He does the heart work. Let us trust and rest in His grace to use our best efforts to do His best for our children.

Questions for Discussion

1. What is discipline? How do you define it? How does the Bible define it?

2. How have you seen your Father in heaven discipline you? What have you learned from that discipline? Are there lessons you've had to repeat? How does your understanding of God's discipline shape how you respond to the sin in your children?

3. Do you ever hesitate to correct your children? Why do you think that is? Why does the Bible teach us that discipline is loving and necessary?

4. Read how Jesus responded to Peter's sin in John 21:15–19 after he denied knowing Him. How would you describe this kind of training?

5. How does understanding your sin nature, and that of your children, impact your expectations of your children? How about your responses to their sin?

6. Do you talk about the gospel when you correct your children? Why or why not? What role should it play in your discipline?

7. How can you image God as you discipline your children today?

A Parent's Prayer

Father in heaven, You are such a good Father! I thank You for how You have trained me. You are loving and gracious. You protect me from evil and lead me back when I've wandered from You. When You bring hardship or suffering into my life, it serves to transform me into the image of Christ. Help me as I parent my own children to see the important role discipline plays in both my life and in the life of my children. Help me to image You as I respond to their sin. Grant me wisdom to provide the proper correction, training, and discipline they need, pointing their hearts to You and Your love for them in Christ.

In Jesus' name, amen.

7

GOD GIVES US WHAT WE NEED

Please? Everyone else has one. Literally. Everyone. Why can't you say yes?"

This was a frequent refrain of mine throughout adolescence. I wanted what everyone else had. I wanted to go where everyone else went. I wanted to watch and listen to what everyone else watched and listened to. More often than not, my parents said no to my repeated pleas. At the time, I believed they were being unfair, out of touch, even cruel. Eventually, I grew up and realized that in saying no they were protecting me from myself.

In my home, the questions I receive are not usually related to purchasing items, though occasionally that happens. More often than not, the questions center around the amount of time I permit my children to play video games or allow them to be on their computers or phones. That's because everyone else seems to play more than they do or is allowed to play certain games I don't permit them play.

I understand this desire to have what others have for my own heart has the same yearning. We all are prone to comparison. We look at others around us and contrast our lives and circumstances to theirs. Inevitably, our life pales in comparison. Someone always has something better: a bigger house, a more attentive spouse, better behaved children, more frequent vacations. Someone else always seems to have it together. They don't appear to have the same struggles or hardships. They live the life we wish we had. And, like a child who gets two pieces of candy compared to her friend who receives three, we think in our hearts, *It's not fair!* and wonder why God hasn't provided for us in the way He has for someone else.

In this chapter, we will look at how our Father in heaven meets our needs, not necessarily our wants. We will look at how He is our perfect provider, giving us the very thing we need most: Himself. As we consider how our Father provides what we need, it helps us as parents make decisions about what we provide for our own children.

Jehovah Jireh, Our Provider

When I was a teen, I helped lead the singing at my youth group's weekly gatherings. I enjoyed choosing the songs we would sing each Friday night. One song we often sang was called "Jehovah-Jireh."[1]

The words about God's grace being sufficient for me and God providing all that I need spoke to me at a time in my life when my family struggled financially. I was often hungry and worried about having the basics in life. I looked ahead to the unknown future and wondered if there would be enough. I learned during those years to cry out to God, whose name Jehovah Jireh means "the Lord will provide." This name comes from the story of Abraham and Isaac in Genesis 22. God told Abraham to take his beloved son Isaac up to Mount Moriah and offer him as a sacrifice. On this same mount the temple would later stand, the place where God would dwell with His people. As Abraham and Isaac trekked up the hillside, Isaac asked his father where the animal was they were to sacrifice. Abraham told him the Lord would provide the sacrifice (v. 8). Every time I read this story, I wonder what thoughts went through Abraham's mind as he trudged up that mountain, knowing he had to sacrifice the child he and Sarah had longed for—the child God gave them when they were far beyond childbearing age, the child of promise. With each step forward, did Abraham cling to God's covenant that he would be the father of many nations? Did he hope God would somehow provide another way? Hebrews 11 tells us Abraham brought Isaac up that mountain by faith for, "He considered that God was able even to raise him from the dead, from which, figuratively speaking, he did receive him back" (v. 19).

Abraham then built an altar and bound Isaac to the top. As he was about to sacrifice Isaac, the angel of the Lord stopped him and said, "Do not lay your hand on the boy or do anything to him, for now I know that you fear God, seeing you have not withheld your son, your only son, from me" (Gen. 22:12). Abraham then looked up and saw a ram caught in a thicket. He took the ram and used it as an offering to God, in the place of Isaac. Abraham then named the place, Jehovah Jireh, "So Abraham called the name of that place, 'The LORD will provide'; as it is said to this day, 'On the mount of the Lord it shall be provided'" (Gen. 22:14). God provided what He required from Abraham; He provided a ram for the sacrifice. Centuries later, God would do the same for us when He provided His only Son to die on the cross for our sins.

Our God is Jehovah Jireh. He is our provider. The word "jireh" also means "to see." God saw our greatest need—redemption from sin—and provided for it. He met our need with a spotless lamb, Jesus Christ, sacrificed in our place. In Romans 8, Paul asks, "He who did not spare his own Son but gave him up for us all, how will he not also with him graciously give us all things?" (v. 32). This is an argument from greater to lesser. Since God provided for our greatest need, how could we think He would not meet all our other needs? This is an important question to ask ourselves when we have worries and concerns about our needs. It reminds us that God is indeed a perfect provider.

Our Father Provides for Our Needs

A few years ago, our family went on an epic trip to Israel. We saw the places we've read about so many times in Scripture. We walked where Jesus walked. We prayed and sang in the same places He prayed and sang. One such location we toured was the hillside where Jesus taught the Sermon on the Mount. Our group sat there, taking in the view of the valley and thinking about the thousands gathered to hear Jesus preach so many centuries before. We took turns reading aloud portions from Matthew 5–7. It is a memory deeply imprinted in my mind and one I recall every time I read this section of Scripture.

One of my favorite portions of this sermon is found in Matthew 6:25–34 where Jesus talks about the worries and cares of this life. It is a tender and compassionate passage, spoken by the One who left the glories of heaven to take on human flesh and experience all the trials and hardships of life in this fallen world. In just a couple of chapters before this, we read of Jesus' encounter with Satan in the wilderness where He fasted for forty days, was tempted to sin, and resisted. Weakened by hunger and thirst, our Savior stood firm against Satan's lies, drawing strength from the Word of God. It is this Jesus—our high priest who is familiar with our weaknesses, the One born in a humble manger, a simple carpenter—who speaks to us about the worries of life.

For many believers, this Matthew 6 passage is a familiar one. It's one we might quickly skim or read through because we know it so well. But it is a beautiful passage, one that we should savor and treasure. Jesus begins by telling His listeners, "Do not be anxious about your life, what you will eat or what you will drink, nor about your body, what you will put on" (Matt. 6:25). The late British pastor Martyn Lloyd-Jones points out that Jesus is referencing the whole of life here, "our health, our strength, our success, what is going to happen to us. . . . And equally takes the body as a whole."[2] Consider all those things we fret and worry over regarding our lives and our health. All those things that consume our time and attention. All those "what if?" questions of the future. Jesus then argues from greater to lesser, "Is not life more than food, and the body more than clothing?" (v. 25). Lloyd-Jones says Jesus wants us to remember where our lives come from, the source of our life. "So the argument which our Lord uses is this. If God has given you the gift of life—the greater gift—do you think He is now suddenly going to deny Himself and His own methods, and not see to it that that life is sustained and enabled to continue?"[3]

Jesus continues by calling our attention to those things we see every day: the birds of the air and the wildflowers of the field. He points out how God provides food for the birds (v. 26) and that the flowers are dressed in finery far greater than that of Solomon (vv. 28–29). Elsewhere in Scripture, we see how God cares for all His creation: "From your lofty abode you water the mountains; the earth is satisfied with the fruit of your work. . . . The young lions roar for their prey, seeking their food from God" (Ps. 104:13, 21). "Are not two sparrows sold for a penny? And not one of them will fall to the ground apart from your Father" (Matt. 10:29). Jesus asks, "Are you not of more value than they?" (Matt. 6:26). God isn't simply a Creator to us, as He is to the animals and plants. He is more; He is our Father. This is an argument from lesser to greater: If God provides for the needs of His creation, how much more will He meet the needs of His beloved children whom He chose in Christ before the creation of the world?

Jesus goes on to say that those who are not God's children, those outside of the faith, worry and stress and fret about their needs, but we have no need to do that. "For the Gentiles seek after all these things, and your heavenly Father knows that you need them all" (v. 32). We are reminded again that God is our Father. He loves and cares for us and knows about all our needs. In fact, our Father knows what we need before we do. He knows everything about us (Ps. 139). He knows our thoughts and desires, our heartaches and fears. He knows our worries and the things that keep us up at night. He knows the temptations we face and the trials we endure. He knows about that job loss and our concerns about our child's education. He knows about the follow-up tests at the doctor's next week and all the bills we need to pay. Our Father knows it all and He promises to meet our needs. Lloyd-Jones concludes: "When you see yourself as His child, then you will know that God will inevitably care for you."[4]

God Doesn't Always Give Us What We Want

After reading all this, you may think, "Yes, I agree that God provides for me. But what about _____?" What about the prayers God has not answered? What about times when He has not given us what we asked for? What about the trial we are in right now that He has not delivered us from? What about the job we lost or the bills we've yet to pay? What about our child's ongoing health struggle? These are important questions and ones we all ask.

Sometimes we read God's promises in Scripture to provide for us and are tempted to think it means He's like a heavenly candy machine: we insert prayer and out come all the things we want. We might then treat Him like a wishing well, tossing prayers like coins for every desire of our heart. But that's not who God is to us; He is not a genie in a lamp popping out to grant us our three greatest wishes. As we've looked at throughout this book, God is our Father, our Maker, our Savior. Yes, He provides for us what we need, but He doesn't always give us what we want. In fact, He gives us more.

> *God provides for us what we need, but He doesn't always give us what we want. In fact, He gives us more.*

The early church father St. Augustine had many desires and wants. Before he came to faith in Christ, he pursued those desires with gusto. He feasted on all the pleasures this world has to offer and worshiped the idols of sex, knowledge, comfort, and alcohol. He tried out various religions and relationships. But none of them satisfied the longing in his soul. After he came to faith, he wrote this now famous quote: "Thou madest us for Thyself, and our heart is restless, until it repose in Thee."[5] We were created to be in relationship with the One who made us and nothing else will satisfy. We can try to fill that void with material things, with relationships, with money and success, but our hearts will remain restless until we are in communion with God, for He is what we need most.

The Jews during Jesus' day longed for the Messiah to come and rescue them. They expected Him to come like a king and take back the power the Romans had taken from them. They expected Him to come like a warrior and conquer their enemies. Instead, Jesus came into this world as a baby born not in a palace, but in a manger. He lived in poverty and never owned a home of His own. His mission was not to take political control; rather, His mission was to redeem sinners. He came to bring us back into fellowship with God, to restore our broken relationship with Him. Instead of conquering a military power, He conquered sin and death. The Jews thought they knew what they needed most, but God knew their greatest need wasn't found in their circumstances here on earth, but in a transformed life and heart. This is true for us. Our greatest need isn't a new job, though often that is a good thing. Our greatest need isn't to pay off financial debt, though that too is a good thing. Our greatest need isn't found in who we marry or what school our child attends or in the successes we have in life or in who wins an election, though those are all good and important things. Our greatest need is not physical, but spiritual. Our greatest need is to be made right with God.

Sometimes, when we pray and ask our Father to provide us something, it may be that what we've prayed for isn't the best thing for us right now. As we've already explored, God uses trials and challenges of life to sanctify us, to teach us, and ultimately, to make us more like Christ. Our Father knows what is best for us, and He will give us all that is good and right and consistent with His will for us. Our task is to pray to our Father for all our needs and then to trust Him to provide for us, knowing that sometimes He has something even better planned for us. As Jesus said in Matthew 7:8–11:

> "For everyone who asks receives, and the one who seeks finds, and to the one who knocks it will be opened. Or

which one of you, if his son asks him for bread, will give him a stone? Or if he asks for a fish, will give him a serpent? If you then, who are evil, know how to give good gifts to your children, how much more will your Father who is in heaven give good things to those who ask him!"

So let us pray to our Father to meet our needs, knowing He always gives us exactly what we need.

Our Father cares for His children. He is a perfect provider. He meets our daily needs. Even more, He's met our greatest need by giving us Jesus Christ. How can we as parents image Jehovah Jireh to our children? How can we show our Father to our children in the way we provide for their needs?

Imaging God to Our Children

What do your children need? That's a big question, isn't it? They need many things. They need love and care. They need instruction and discipline. They need safety and security. They need food and shelter. They need all the things we've discussed so far in this book. And as parents, we are responsible to provide those needs. Certainly, we are responsible legally, but even more, we are responsible to God to care for our children's needs. We are their first providers, and in meeting their needs, we point our children to their Father in heaven.

The Bible often compares a parent's care for their children to how God cares for us:

"As a father shows compassion to his children, so the LORD shows compassion to those who fear him." (Ps. 103:13)

"Can a woman forget her nursing child, that she should have no compassion on the son of her womb? Even these may forget, yet I will not forget you." (Isa. 49:15)

"As one whom his mother comforts, so I will comfort you; you shall be comforted in Jerusalem." (Isa. 66:13)

"But we were gentle among you, like a nursing mother taking care of her own children." (1 Thess. 2:7)

As we provide for and meet our children's needs, they see the Father through us. As parents, we often put time and effort into making their meals each day. We might cut the crust off the bread, just the way they prefer their PB&J. Or we make their favorite meal three days in a row, because they really only eat three things! Or we might get creative with meal prep, looking for ways to add extra nutrition into the meals they do like to eat. In all these ways, we show our children the Father who provides our daily bread. When you stay up all night to comfort your frightened child during a scary thunderstorm, she sees the Father who is the God of all comfort, who shelters us in the storms of life. When you care for your son during an illness and take him to the doctor for checkups, he sees the Father who is the Great Physician and healer of our souls. In your efforts to provide for children's educational needs and in teaching them about this great big world God has made, they see the Father who is the source of all wisdom. And when you provide nourishing love and affection to our children, they see the Father who loved them in Christ before time began.

Wants vs. Needs

But just like our own wants and needs are not always the same, this is true for our children as well. What they need isn't always the same as what they want. What about when our children ask for something we don't think is good for them? What about when they just want what everyone else has? What about when we truly just can't provide something for them because of a limited budget? Just as God always gives us what we need, but not necessarily what we want, there are times we do the same with our children.

We parents always want to provide more for our children than we had as children. We want our children to have opportunities, experiences, and resources we didn't have available to us in our childhood. I know I do. That's why my husband and I have taken our children on trips to see places we never saw as children. It's why we've exposed them to team sports at a young age. It's why we've provided certain educational opportunities, read numerous books to them, and encouraged them in their natural skills and abilities. While there is nothing wrong with wanting more for our children than we had, we must pause and remember how God parents us.

Consider those things God taught you from a place of lacking. During those times when you didn't have resources or access to something, you learned to depend and rely on God in ways you wouldn't have learned otherwise. There are numerous times in my life where I didn't have enough money, or skill, or strength and the Lord met me there with exactly what I needed. I often look back on those times to remind myself of His provision. Think too about those times you failed at something and learned that your value and worth is not found in your successes but in who you are in Christ. Or those occasions when God didn't give you what you prayed for right away and you learned patience and hope while waiting. Or when God placed an obstacle in your path so you could not get that job or house or other thing you desired and as a result, you realized how much that thing was an idol you worshiped, and it brought you to repentance. In all these ways and more, when God doesn't give us everything we want or brings us through challenging circumstances, He provides us what we need to learn and grow in our faith.

In the book of Proverbs, the author asks God not to give him too much or too little, "give me neither poverty nor riches; feed me with the food that is needful for me, lest I be full and deny you and say, 'Who is the LORD?' or lest I be poor and steal and profane the name of my God" (30:8–9). He describes how either extreme is problematic to his relationship with the Lord. There is wisdom here for us as we consider what we provide for our children. A good place to start is with prayer, asking for wisdom to know what is good and needed for our children. In terms of material goods, we might decide not to buy them everything they ask for. Or we may intentionally allow them to learn to wait for something. There's no formula for such things, only wisdom gleaned from God and His Word.

Ultimately, we want to provide for our children their greatest need: redemption in Christ. While only God can provide that for them, we are to point them to that need and to the God who fulfills it. When this is our priority, it helps other things fall into place. We can measure the opportunities and experiences and material things we consider "provision" against this need. How might a particular experience help or hinder their relationship with God? How might a specific activity be a barrier or pathway to their grasp of the gospel? How might the pursuit of a material item conflict with or help them see Christ as their greatest need?

The Importance of Saying No

Our children do not yet know what is best for them. They do not have the knowledge, experience, and maturity to make decisions for themselves. Throughout childhood, they will gain the knowledge necessary to do so by the time they are adults. God has made us the authority in their lives, and they are to obey that authority—for when they do so, they obey God Himself.

This means we need to be comfortable with saying no when necessary. There are times when our children ask for something and we know it is not good for them so we have to say no. They may argue or resist or complain but we need to be firm in our decision. When we give in to requests simply to placate them or to keep them from having an angry outburst in public, our children learn their response was acceptable and before long, they respond in kind every time we say no.

However, it is also important that when we say no to something, it is for the right reason. Sometimes, we say no because we don't want to be inconvenienced or because we don't want to take the time to truly consider their request. There are times when I'm tired at the end of the day and just want to spend the evening relaxing and doing what I want to do. But then one of my children asks me for a ride somewhere and I immediately want to say, "No." The request is an interruption to my plans. Children can quickly identify if we turn down a request out of our own selfishness or laziness. This is an opportunity for us to model how God responds to our requests. When we have a need, we cry out to God in prayer. He listens to us and provides for what we need. May we do the same for our children. May we listen to our children when they come to us. May they find us accessible and always ready to hear what they have to say. May they see us as parents who seek to provide what is best for them, as our Father does for us.

Modeling to Our Children

There have been times in our own family when we could not provide everything our children needed. Perhaps our budget was tight, or we simply lacked the wisdom to make the right decision. We then prayed together as a family for the Lord to provide what we needed. Maybe we prayed for financial help, for wisdom to know the way, or for the Lord to help us be content with His provision. Such prayers help our children learn to cry out to God for their own needs.

Our children learn much from listening to us pray aloud. They learn that God is the source of all good things and that all we have comes from His hand. They learn to seek Him for their daily bread and to turn to Him for comfort, deliverance, and healing.

When our children were young, we had a jar filled with popsicle sticks on the table. On each stick we wrote a prayer request. These were requests for not only our own family, but also for others we were praying for. We then took turns at mealtimes praying aloud for these needs. Whoever's turn it was to pray would grab a stick and pray for that need. We used this as a tool to help our children learn to pray aloud and to develop the practice of praying to the Lord for their needs. These days, we continue to take turns praying at the dinner table, bringing our requests to our Jehovah Jireh, the One who provides for all that we need.

Questions for Discussion

1. Read Philippians 4:6. What is your greatest need right now? Have you prayed to your Father about it?

2. How have you seen God meet your needs in the past? Have there been times when God did not give you what you wanted but gave you something else instead? What have you learned from those times when God did not give you what you asked for?

3. Read Psalm 37:4. When does God give us the desires of our heart?

4. Read Proverbs 30:7-9. What do you think of this request? What can you glean from this passage for how you provide for your children?

5. What do your children need most? In what ways would they benefit from you saying no to something they want?

6. What are some practical ways you can teach your children that God is Jehovah Jireh?

7. What are some ways you can image your Father in heaven to your children today?

A Parent's Prayer

Jehovah Jireh, You are my provider. You meet all my needs. You know all my needs before I even ask for them. I thank You for the gift of faith in Christ. You made a way for me to be restored to relationship with You. You always make a way. Help me to remember the promise and provision of Abraham and know You always provide. As I consider all the ways You provide for me, help me to image You to my children in my provisions for them. It is so hard to not buy them everything they want! It is so hard to say no to their requests. Help me to measure all things against their soul's greatest need for You. May my provisions for them point them to You, their Jehovah Jireh.

In Jesus' name, amen.

8

GOD IS PATIENT WITH HIS CHILDREN

When you first have a child, friends and family often share stories of their own parenting experiences. They also give advice about everything from favorite gadgets and toys to the best way to get a baby to sleep through the night. One piece of advice I heard from multiple parents was, "Enjoy every moment because it goes by so fast." Each of these friends were ahead of me in the parenting journey. They likely looked down at my son snug in his car carrier and remembered when their children were small enough to carry around—children who had since grown up and left home.

While I listened to their advice, I wasn't so quick to follow it. I was impatient for my boys to grow. Instead of enjoying the current stage they were in, I looked forward to the next. I kept thinking, "I can't wait until he sleeps through the night. Then we all can get some sleep too." "I can't wait until he can walk on his own, so I don't have to carry him." "I can't wait until he can talk . . . is potty-trained . . . can ride a bike . . . can drive a car." Soon enough, I found myself passing on the same wisdom once shared with me, having learned the hard way that time does pass all too quickly.

But my impatience went further than just wanting to push fast-forward on the passage of time. I was also impatient with my children's unique idiosyncrasies; the way they insisted on things being a certain way; their constant energy and curiosity; their resistance to change. I was also impatient with their behavior. I grew irritated when I had to repeat the same instruction or teach the same lesson. I found myself saying, "How many times do I have to tell you to . . .?" I responded in frustration over normal childish behavior—excessive excitement, mishaps, and general forgetfulness. As a result, one of my most fervent prayers was for patience. (Incidentally, it's been a prayer I've heard my own children pray for me!) My patience has been tested more as a parent than in any other context. It truly has been a place in my life where the Lord's sanctifying work is most active.

Patience is one of those qualities we pray for; yet, when the Lord provides us opportunities to learn and practice it, we resist the opportunity. It's a bit like exercise: Wouldn't it be nice to just wake up one day all toned and strong without having to do the work to get there? We'd like to be given patience on a silver platter, not have to practice it in the face of frustrating experiences. Patience also seems elusive, just out of reach. We know what it looks like when we see it, but to grasp it seems impossible. It's like trying to catch a hummingbird midflight; it darts away as quickly as it arrived.

Our struggle with patience can look different from one person to the next. Some may struggle with the rapid-fire questions a three-year-old asks. Others are impatient with having to remind their children to do tasks they should have learned long ago.

Some simply find a child's immaturity and incessant curiosity frustrating. Still others find themselves most impatient with their child who has such a different personality than their own. When we are impatient, we might respond to our children with irritation and annoyance. We might be sarcastic and belittling. We may even respond in outright anger. Impatience creates a barrier in our relationship with our children. Even more, we know the Bible calls us to patience with one another (1 Cor. 13:4; Gal. 5:22; 1 Thess. 5:14).

Over the years of parenting, I kept coming back to my own impatience, looking at it from different angles and dissecting it. I wanted to be more patient, but it seemed so hard and I started to wonder if maybe I just wasn't capable of it. Yet, as my children grew into the preteen years, the Lord gently reminded me of my own preteen years. Like Dickens' tale, I revisited my past and saw how the Lord was patient with me throughout my life. I started to see the slow process of sanctification in my life—the starts and stops, the lessons learned and repeated, and how the Lord was long-suffering with me in that process. And the more I thought about my Father's patience with me, I found my own impatience with my children start to recede.

In this chapter, we'll look at God's patience for us and how it shapes our own patience with our children.

God Is Patient

One of God's characteristics is that He is patient. The patience God has for us is a bit different than how we usually think of patience. I often think of patience as the quality of waiting in line without getting irritated. Or overlooking the unique mannerisms of people in my life. Or even just enduring the passage of time until an event

I look forward to takes place. And certainly, patience does mean that. But in the Bible, there's an even deeper nuance to this characteristic, especially when it describes God's patience with us.

When Moses asked to see God's glory, God passed before him and described Himself as "merciful and gracious, slow to anger, and abounding in steadfast love and faithfulness" (Ex. 34:6). This description of God is repeated throughout the Old Testament. That phrase "slow to anger" is translated as *long-suffering* in the King James, another word for patience. Long-suffering means to patiently endure lasting offense for the sake of love. The prophet Jonah knew this characteristic of God and that is why he didn't want to go to Nineveh and instead attempted to run away (Jonah 4:2). Throughout the Old Testament, we read account after account of Israel's sin and God's great patience or long-suffering. He sent multiple prophets to preach repentance and warn them of the consequences of their sin. He withheld the punishment they were due and gave them opportunities to turn from their sin and back to Him. God suffered long; He was patient for the sake of love. And so He is with us.

Consider the Lord's patience toward us before we came to faith in Christ and the lives we lived. Examine the ways we lived for ourselves, worshiped false gods, and trampled on the truth. Consider also our sinful thoughts, words, and deeds. God patiently endured our sin until the time when He opened our eyes to see our need for a Savior. He saved us from our sin, brought us into the family of God, and trained us in the way of righteousness. Though we are no longer slaves to sin and are freed from its power over us, its presence still remains. The Lord continues to be patient with us as we learn and relearn the way of grace. Time and again, we sin and seek forgiveness through the blood of Christ and God forgives us. He suffers long for the sake of love for us. What grace!

The apostle Paul reminds us of God's patience with us when he calls us to put on patience ourselves. "Put on then, as God's chosen ones, holy and beloved, compassionate hearts, kindness, humility, meekness, and patience, bearing with one another and, if one has a complaint against another, forgiving each other; as the Lord has forgiven you, so you also must forgive" (Col. 3:12–13). We are to love others the way God loves us. We are to be patient and long-suffering. We are to forgive as we've been forgiven. The Puritan preacher Jonathan Edwards describes this long-suffering love for others: "He, therefore, that exercises a Christian long-suffering toward his neighbor, will bear the injuries received from him without revenging or retaliating, either by injurious deeds or bitter words. . . . He will receive all with a calm, undisturbed countenance, and with a soul full of meekness, quietness, and goodness."[1]

God Is Patient as We Grow

One of the ways God is patient with us is in our growth in faith. He is like a patient gardener, tending His garden and waiting for the harvest.

One year in homeschooling, my children and I did a study on botany. For those who are unfamiliar with homeschooling, parents often learn just as much as the children, and this was true in our study of plants. We did an experiment with seeds, wrapping them in a wet paper towel and placing them in a few different plastic bags. We then placed those bags in various places around the house to see where the seeds thrived most. No surprise, they did not do well when placed at the top of the schoolroom closet! During that year, we studied all kinds of plants, learned how they grew, and observed various plants throughout the growth process. Unfortunately, I also relearned that I did not inherit my grandfather's green thumb.

The Bible uses many agrarian and agricultural metaphors to describe spiritual concepts. In ancient history, people understood these metaphors because most people grew the food they ate. They didn't drive to their local grocery to select their melons and cucumbers from a stack in the produce section. They also knew firsthand the work involved in tending vineyards. They knew what a healthy fruit-bearing tree looked like and what it took for that tree to bear fruit. They knew too how their wheat grew, how to grind it into flour, and then how bake it into the bread they ate.

That's why there are so many references to plants, gardens, vines, and fruit in Scripture. In John 15, Jesus describes Himself as a vine, we as the branches, and the Father as the gardener:

> "I am the true vine, and my Father is the vinedresser. Every branch in me that does not bear fruit he takes away, and every branch that does bear fruit he prunes, that it may bear more fruit. Already you are clean because of the word that I have spoken to you. Abide in me, and I in you. As the branch cannot bear fruit by itself, unless it abides in the vine, neither can you, unless you abide in me. I am the vine; you are the branches. Whoever abides in me and I in him, he it is that bears much fruit, for apart from me you can do nothing." (John 15:1–5)

Jesus uses this imagery to compare our growth as Christians to that of a vineyard. Just as a branch receives nourishment from the vine in order to grow and thrive, we receive spiritual nourishment through our union with Christ. Just as a branch can't grow on its own apart from the vine, we can't do anything apart from Christ. Just as a gardener tends to his plants, trimming and pruning them, so too does God prune us so that we can produce more fruit. Though most of us do not grow grapes, we have a rudimentary understanding of how things grow and can learn from this passage about our own growth in the faith.

When we consider all that takes place in the life of a plant—from the seed planted in the ground to the harvest of fruit—it is quite a process. A long process. The plant's growth does not happen overnight. There are many days of quiet underground before the first shoot makes an appearance. This infant plant must continue to grow before it is ready to bear fruit. The gardener ensures it is watered and fertilized. The sun shines down its nutrients. The plant continues to grow. It endures dark days and ferocious storms. It continues to grow. One spring day, buds appear. Then flowers. Then finally the fruit and, with it, the harvest.

Our Father is a patient gardener, tilling the soil of our heart. He plants seeds of faith in us and nourishes us with His Word. He watches over us with love and care. He doesn't rush the process, knowing that our growth takes time. He tends to our hearts, pruning and trimming away what doesn't belong. He protects us from evil pests that threaten our growth. He doesn't leave us on our own; He keeps us in the vine through all the storms of life. He finishes what He starts in us and ensures we bear the fruit of righteousness.

Imaging God in Patience

The Bible teaches us to be patient with others just as our Father is patient with us. Patience is one of God's characteristics. He is slow to anger. He is merciful and does not give us what we deserve. We've seen how He was patient with us before we came to faith. We've seen how He is long-suffering because of His great love for us. We've seen how He patiently teaches and trains and nurtures us. As God's image bearers, we are called to reflect the patience God has for us to others, including our children.

First though, it's important that we remember that patience is a fruit. It is not something we come by naturally. We can't simply muster it up by sheer will power. It grows and develops in us by the work of the Spirit. As Paul wrote in Galatians 5:22–23, "But the fruit of the Spirit is love, joy, peace, patience, kindness, goodness, faithfulness, gentleness, self-control; against such things there is no law." In the John 15 passage above, Jesus said that we bear fruit out of our union with Him. As we abide in Him through the Word and prayer, as we grow in our faith, we'll see the fruit of patience develop in our lives. This is good

As God's image bearers, we are called to reflect the patience God has for us to others, including our children.

news for those of us who have tried in our own strength to be patient and have failed. This also means patience isn't as elusive as it seems. It *is* within reach—through the power and work of the Holy Spirit. Let us pray for this fruit to develop in our lives.

What are some areas where we can practice the fruit of patience with our children, showing them the Father, our patient Gardener?

Patience in Development

Those who work with children—doctors, teachers, therapists—know that children learn certain things at certain times in their development. Children grow incrementally throughout the growing process. They are capable of certain physical tasks at certain times. They move from rolling to crawling to walking to running. They understand speech before they speak it themselves. Their thinking is concrete before it is logical. It is not a process that can be rushed. And even when they've started to learn something, it takes time before that lesson is fully learned. A child who has started walking will not walk with certainty for some time; for a while he will stumble and fall. A child who has learned to read will continue to struggle over more complex words until they are mastered.

This means we must be patient at each stage in our child's development, not expecting more of them than they are capable and not expecting them to master something right away. Just because they are physically capable of picking up their toys, it doesn't mean they are emotionally or mentally mature enough to know the right timing in doing so or even the best organizational methods to do so. There are tasks we will need to do with them over and over before they are mastered.

It also takes time before a child can juggle multiple tasks in their mind at once. You may send your daughter to her room with the instruction to get dressed for the day, make her bed, and brush her teeth and she may return having only completed one task. You may respond in exasperation because you know she can do all three tasks on her own. She can, just not all at once. She will need to receive one instruction at a time. Your preteen son may be capable of completing the homework assignments he is given, but he may have difficulty organizing his time well in order to accomplish all those assignments before they are due. He may be overwhelmed by juggling multiple tasks and due dates and forget something important in the process. He needs help and instruction in organizing his time, prioritizing tasks, and keeping track of when his assignments are due.

A person's brain hasn't finished developing until they are in their early twenties. This means we can't expect our children to think, behave, and respond as an adult would until that time. This can be frustrating to parents, especially in the teenage years when our children appear mature on the outside. They may stand a foot taller than we do and look like a young adult, but their brain is still growing and maturing. We can't be surprised by teens who make impulsive decisions or who lose track of time or who need to be reminded about things. They continue to need our guidance and reminders. They need patient parents who walk alongside them, teaching—then re-teaching—how to navigate the world.

We show patience to our children as we help them with tasks and don't respond with irritation when they need help or reminders. Patience is displayed when we don't expect more from them than they are capable of. Or, when we don't respond with anger or sarcasm when they stumble, make a mistake, or forget something they already know. Parents must be like gardeners who patiently wait and watch as the seed grows in the soil. Our Father, the Gardener, is patient with us as we grow. May we reflect Him as we patiently wait for our children to grow and mature.

Patience in Behavior

If you search the phrase "slow to anger" in a Bible app, you'll find numerous citations describing God as slow to anger. Impatience and anger go hand in hand. When we are impatient with our children's behavior, we may respond to them in anger or be harsh in our words and actions. We'll say unkind things and may belittle them with sarcasm. We will threaten them with extreme consequences. The Bible cautions us to not be quick to become angry (Eccl. 7:9; Eph. 4:26, 31; James 1:19–20), nor to sin in our anger. Many of us have lashed out at our children in anger. We know it is wrong, but find ourselves so exasperated and frustrated, we react to their behavior.

If we dig beneath that anger, we often find the idol of control lurking there. Impatience desires control over time, circumstances, and people. We want things to happen on our schedule and timetable. We want life to go the way we plan. We want people to do things our way. The more we worship control, the more we find ourselves angry at the slow person in traffic or the long wait at the checkout lane. We are quickly frustrated when unexpected events cut into our carefully planned day.

When it comes to our children, we respond in anger when we cannot control their behavior. Whether they are slow getting out the door in the morning, making us late to work; their fatigued cries make it difficult for us to get any shopping done; or their repeated troubles in the classroom require yet another meeting with the teacher, we can find ourselves impatient and angry. We just want them to do what we want them to do. We just want things to go as we've planned. Often, our anger comes not because our children are violating the law of God, but because they are not keeping ours. Our wants and desires take precedence, and when they are broken, we lose our patience.

Instead, God calls us to respond with patience, with long-suffering. We do so because we know God has rescued and forgiven us for far worse than anything our children have done. We know how many times we stumble into the same sin, and yet God forgives us through the blood of Christ. We know our own wandering hearts and how easily distracted we are. We know our own immaturity and how far we've yet to go in our own growth and development. As Paul Tripp wrote, "Like our children, you and I do the same wrong things over and over again because we are not only blind, but we are blind to our blindness. We need compassionate, patient care if we are ever going to change, and so do our children."[2] We can't be like the unmerciful servant in the parable who was forgiven much for his debt but who then went on and imprisoned those who owed him little (Matt. 18:21–35). We must be slow to anger and quick to forgive.

Sometimes this means stepping away from our children and not interacting with them until we've calmed down. We might need to refrain from making any decisions about discipline until later. Patience might also look like not putting things off until the last minute so that we find ourselves rushing around and being frustrated with our children because they don't rush alongside us. Perhaps we need to reevaluate our expectations for our children. Do we expect something they aren't capable of doing yet? Are they too young to drag from one errand to another without a nap in between? We might also need to take an honest look at our heart for idols and ask ourselves: Are we impatient and angry because our children are violating God's Word, or because they have violated our own personal laws and expectations?

Patience also requires being proactive rather than reactionary. We are more likely to be impatient when we've not anticipated or planned for a challenge. After too many tortuously long visits to the doctor's office with my children, I learned to bring extra snacks, activity books, and small toys for my busy boys. One time when the doctor finally arrived to our exam room, he found that they turned the entire space into a racetrack for their cars! It was worth taking the extra time to prepare because rather than whine or fuss—and me respond with impatience—my children were contentedly busy as we waited for the doctor.

In whatever ways we practically live out patience in our parenting, may those ways be rooted in our Father's patience and grace toward us. May we all take time to remember His great long-suffering for us.

Patience in Waiting for God to Work

Another area that is difficult for parents to be patient in is waiting for the Lord to work in their child's heart. As believers, our greatest desire is to see our children come to faith in Christ. We long to see them join the family of God, to trust in Jesus as their Savior, and to know we will be with them in eternity. This is a good and right longing. Yet, it is hard to wait and watch for the Lord to work in our children's hearts to bring them from death to life in Christ.

One of the inherent characteristics of patience is waiting well. When it comes to waiting for the Lord to work in our children's hearts, we need to wait with hope and confidence. The Bible tells us that it is good to wait for the Lord, "It is good that one should wait quietly for the salvation of the LORD" (Lam. 3:26). That's because good things happen as we wait. Our own hearts are changed in the process as we rest in the Lord's sovereignty and trust in His faithfulness. We learn to depend on Him. We are reminded of our human limitations and of our great need for God and His grace.

Yet, as we wait on the Lord, it doesn't mean we don't do anything. It's not like sitting in the waiting room at the doctor's office, twiddling our thumbs or playing endless games of solitaire. There is such a thing as active waiting. While we wait, we cry out to the Lord in prayer (Ps. 40:1). We hope in His Word (Ps. 130:5). Our heart takes courage (Ps. 27:14). We continue to move forward in our calling as parents, teaching and training our children in God's Word. We continue to point them to the gospel. We continue to show them their Father in heaven. Like a gardener, we tend our garden, and wait for the Lord to bring in the harvest.

As we've looked at the characteristic of patience in this chapter, I hope that you've reflected on your Father's patience with you. May His patience shape your own patience with your children.

Questions for Discussion

1. How has your Father shown patience to you in your life?

2. Read Romans 8:18–25 and James 5:7–11. How is patience a characteristic of the Christian life, especially as we wait for Christ to return?

3. Read Proverbs 15:18; Ecclesiastes 7:9; Ephesians 4:2–3. How are we to respond to others?

4. Read Colossians 3:12–13. What is the source of our patience?

5. What areas of parenting do you find the most frustrating, where you struggle to be patient with your children? Why do you think that is?

6. Patience and waiting go hand in hand. What can you do while you wait for the Lord to work in the life of your children?

7. How can you image your Father's patience to your children today?

A Parent's Prayer

Father in heaven, I come before You with a heart that is quick to impatience. I've never waited well. I am frustrated by immaturity. I dislike having to remind my children about things they have learned long ago. But then I remember Your great patience with me. You planted the seed of faith in my heart and nurtured it into a young plant. You watered and fed it. You protected it from the storms of life. And You continue to patiently watch me grow and produce fruit. Help me remember Your great patience with me, and may it shape how I respond to my children as they grow.

In Jesus' name, amen.

9

GOD LOVES HIS CHILDREN

I *love you.*

These are just three little words, but how powerful they can be! In our family, these are important words. They are foundational and essential to our relationship with each other. We don't save these words for special occasions, like the cake and ice cream we enjoy on our birthdays. They are more like bread and butter, the basic and essential food for hungry hearts.

We say these three words to each other and to our children every day. It was an intentional move from the start of our marriage. After all, my husband learned at thirteen how precious and fleeting life can be when his father unexpectedly died. As for me, I don't remember hearing these words from anyone in my family until my grandmother died when I was in high school. I *knew* I was loved; they just weren't words people in my family spoke.

But we too learned that words left unspoken can leave one filled with regrets. I didn't know how much my heart hungered for those words until my grandfather said them to me for the first time. Time seemed to freeze for a moment as I savored the words like a piece of my favorite dark chocolate. I wanted the moment to last as long as possible. It was a pivotal experience in my adolescence, meeting a basic human need: A need to know I was loved and cherished. That I was important. That I was accepted and valued no matter what.

But love is more than words. Such words are meaningless if we do not treat other people with love, if we don't *show* love in our actions. This chapter comes at the end of the book for a reason. All the characteristics discussed in the preceding chapters lead and point us to the Father's great love for us. The structure, boundaries, training, discipline, provision, and patience God provides for His children are rooted in His perfect love. In this chapter, we will look at the love God has for us and then how that love shapes our love for our children.

What Is Love?

Love is something people talk about all the time. Songs are sung about it. Movies are centered around it. There's even a holiday devoted to it. But when people use the word "love" just what does it mean? In our culture, the word "love" is most often used to refer to a feeling. It is an emotion that is all-encompassing, almost a power unto itself, one to be followed and obeyed. Songs and movies urge us to "follow our heart" wherever it leads; yet, all too often, the feeling is temporary and fleeting. For many, love comes and goes like the ocean's tide. Once the feeling passes, so too does the relationship. People fall in and out of love like summer shifting into fall. This isn't only true for romantic relationships, for many also have strained, even severed, relationships with family and friends. As years pass by without contact, many cannot even remember what it was that caused the division.

The word "love" is also used for trivial things, such as food, experiences, and sports teams. I don't know about you, but when I drink a good cup of coffee, I praise it and exclaim my love for it. We talk about loving a trip abroad, the latest blockbuster movie, or our newest edition of the smartphone. We often mean that it is something we really enjoy; we are passionate about it. Yet, it won't take long before our love for those things wanes, only to be to replaced by something new and better. How fickle is humanity's love, both for things and for people!

The Bible uses the word "love" a bit differently than our world. When it talks about love, it's not referring to a temporary feeling, but to an action. Biblical love is not fleeting, but eternal. It's not dependent on what the other person does or does not do, for it is unconditional. It isn't focused on what we receive from others, but what we can give to them. The Bible's most famous passage on love describes it as "patient and kind; love does not envy or boast; it is not arrogant or rude. It does not insist on its own way; it is not irritable or resentful; it does not rejoice at wrongdoing, but rejoices with the truth. Love bears all things, believes all things, hopes all things, endures all things" (1 Cor. 13:4–7). These words are often read at weddings. They were printed on my wedding invitations in that burgundy hue so popular in the mid-90s. This passage reveals that love is more than a feeling. It is committed action for the sake of another.

But the Bible has more to say about love. It tells us that love originated in God; He is the source and fountainhead of love. Even more, it teaches us that God is love (1 John 4:8, 16). Throughout the pages of Scripture, we read the depths of God's love for us. Some even describe the Bible as the story of God's love for His people. In terms of the topic of this book, it is God's love for us that transforms and shapes our love for others, including our children.

To understand love, we have to begin at the source: God Himself.

God's Great Love for Us

The early church struggled with a number of theological truths we now take for granted. In the first few centuries after Christ's ascension, the church fathers gathered together in councils to discuss the Bible's teachings on various doctrines, including the nature of Christ. What we understand today as the Trinity was developed during these meetings and the subsequent writings of the fathers.

St. Augustine was one of those early church fathers who helped the church further grasp the Trinity through his work *On the Trinity*. In this lengthy treatise, he was the first to describe the Trinity as a relationship of love between the three persons of the Godhead. The Bible teaches us that God is love. Since love involves a relationship, Augustine reasoned that God must be in a relationship. He argued that because God is perfect, His love must also be perfect; and since only God is perfect, He must love Himself.[1] Further, in order for Him to love Himself, He must have a conception of Himself: the Son, who is the exact image of Himself. Augustine taught that the Holy Spirit also shares in that love; the Spirit is the love that proceeds from the Father and Son and unites them together.

This understanding of the Trinity as a relationship of mutual love helps us understand that love originates in God. God the Father, God the Son, and God the Holy Spirit have existed for all eternity in a relationship of perfect love. This triune relationship was complete and lacked nothing. For all eternity, our Three-in-One God has enjoyed a relationship of mutual love wherein each member of the Godhead honors, glorifies, serves, and cherishes the other. In creating mankind, God invited us to join in this glorious relationship, to participate in and enjoy sweet fellowship with the God of the universe.

The Puritan preacher Jonathan Edwards illustrated this truth in his description of heaven as the nucleus of God's love. "There, even in heaven, dwells the God from whom every stream of holy love, yea, every drop that is, or ever was, proceeds."[2] He described the love of our triune God as a free-flowing fountain, pouring forth love, which swells into an ocean of love, wherein the redeemed bathe with great joy. He described their love for one another: "There dwells God the Father, God the Son, and God the Spirit, united as one, infinitely dear, and incomprehensible, and mutual, and eternal love"[3] and of Christ, the expression of that love, "There dwells the great Mediator, through whom all the divine love is expressed toward men, and by whom the fruits of that love have been purchased, and through whom they are communicated, and through whom love is imparted to the hearts of all God's people."[4] It's amazing isn't it? To think of the holy and perfect love shared between the Father, Son, and Holy Spirit given to us, shared with us, living within us. To think of that love as deep and wide as the ocean. What wonder! It's hard for our minds to comprehend but we will have an eternity to do so.

The picture Edwards paints of God's love is reflected in Scripture. The Bible tells us that God is love. This doesn't mean He is *only* love, for the Bible tells us He is also holy, righteous, merciful, and true. What it does mean is that love is an integral part of God's character; we can't talk about His attributes apart from His love. God is the beginning, source, and wellspring of love. The love the Trinity shares has always existed (John 17:20–26). The Bible tells us that God chose us in love before time began (Eph. 1:4–5). Just think on that for a moment: our triune God thought of us, loved us, and chose us long before the first sunrise, and long before the day of our birth.

Since God is the source of love, we cannot know what love is apart from Him. He is the One who defines it, expresses it, and shares it with us. So, when we want to know what love is, we look to who God is and what He has done. Here are a few things the Bible tells us about God and His love:

- God's love is rooted in His covenant love for His people (Isa. 54).
- God's love is abounding (Ps. 86:15).
- God is the source and initiator of love for us (1 John 4:16; Rom. 5:8).
- God loved us when we did not love Him (Eph. 2:4–5).
- God's love for us was proved in the giving of His Son to die for our sins (John 3:16; 1 John 4:9–10).
- God the Father loves us as much as He loves the Son (John 17:23).
- In God's love, we are His children (1 John 3:1).
- God's love is unfathomable (Eph. 3:18–19).
- God's love resides within us, through the Holy Spirit (Rom. 5:5).
- Nothing can separate us from God's love (Rom. 8:38–39).
- God's love changes and transforms us (Ezek. 36:26; 2 Cor. 5:17).

This chapter cannot even begin to explore all that the Bible tells us about God's love. If this is a topic you have not explored before, I commend you to the study of it.

When I pause to consider God's great love, I can't help but respond in awe and wonder. In the words of Charles Wesley, "Amazing love! How can it be / That thou, my God, shouldst die for me?"[5]

Our Love for Others

As we learned, the indicatives in Scripture inform the imperatives. The truths of who God is and what He has done for us in Christ are what fuels our response to Him. These truths shape how we live. They inform how we engage with others. This means we love others *because* God first loved us. We love others *out* of the love God has for us. We love *as* God has loved us.

The apostle John is known as the disciple whom Jesus loved. In his letters, he wrote in depth about God's love for us and how it shapes our love for others: "Beloved, if God so loved us, we also ought to love one another" (1 John 4:11). The greatest act of love—the sacrifice Jesus made for His people at the cross—is the impetus for our love for others. Because God loved us first, we know how to love others. Apart from God's love, we cannot truly love others. Because of our sin nature, we are naturally selfish creatures. We seek our own interest above others. We harbor anger and resentments against others. Even when we do something kind for another, our motives are impure, tainted by our sin. But because we now know and have experienced God's love for us in Christ, we love others. We know the depths of our sin and the great lengths God went to in rescuing us and making us His children. We know the sacrificial love of Christ on our behalf. We know how much we've been forgiven and the great cost to purchase that forgiveness. We can love others because God first loved us.

As believers, we have the Spirit of Christ living within us. We experience the love of God as the Spirit comforts, guides, and teaches us. He showers us with His love and grace. He sanctifies us to make us more like Christ. He reminds us of the Word of God and applies it to our heart. The more we yield to His work in us, the more we are shaped and transformed by His love. Through the work of the Spirit in us, we are enabled to love others as God loves us. Jesus talked about this as abiding in Him (John 15). John wrote, "If we love one another, God abides in us and his love is perfected in us" (1 John 4:12). Like a branch attached to a vine, we are united to Christ by faith. All that He has is ours. As we abide in Him, we are nourished, just as a branch is fed by the vine. We grow and thrive and bear the fruit of love. We then love others out of the love we receive from God.

We also love others as God has loved us. Jesus' life and death are the standard and model for our love for others. Jesus taught us what love looks like. He instructed us to put others first, to honor others, to serve others. He both taught and demonstrated how to forgive others. In His interactions with others, Jesus showed us how to look past the outward things and into the heart. He also explains that love is sacrificial. He showed us how to love the unloving, how to love our enemies, and how to love unto death. Christian love is defined by the God of love. We love others in the same way we are loved.

As we've seen in this brief look at God's love, He loves us with an immeasurable love. It is a one-way love, initiated by Him. It is not based on anything we have done. He set His love on us in eternity past and made us His own through the death of His Son. It is a love that no one can take away. It is eternal. It is firm and secure. And it is all transforming as He works in us through His Spirit to make us new. The question is, how can we image this love the Father has for us to our children?

Imaging God to Our Children

I've loved my children since I first saw the confirmation on the pregnancy test. Everything changed at that point. I began to think about the life I wanted for them, the kind of parent I wanted to be, and what life would be like as a family. I remember trying to picture what they would look like. What physical characteristics would they inherit from my husband? From me? Setting up their nurseries was a joy as I imagined myself rocking them to sleep or reading bedtime stories or playing games on the floor. I spent hours sitting in the rocking chair praying for them. And as I awaited their arrival, I found myself in Momma Bear mode, doing everything the doctor instructed in order to protect and keep them safe—a mode I continue in today!

Whether you waited nine months for your child to arrive or longer, as you waited through months of adoption paperwork, interviews, and approvals, you also loved your child before you met him or her. But as we all know, because we are fallen sinners, love doesn't always come easy. We don't always love as we ought to. Some of us may not have experienced healthy parental love and while we love our children, we find it hard to show it. Let's explore some important characteristics of love and practical ways to love our children as God loves us.

Unconditional Love

When our children were young, we read them a picture book titled *I'll Love You Anyway and Always* by Bryan Chapell.[6] In the story, a young child did something wrong and her father teaches her that he loves her, even when she has sinned. After reading that story, whenever our children did something wrong and we had to correct them, we would remind them we loved them "anyway and always."

One of the errors our culture makes about love is in its transitory nature. We love something or someone only until something better comes along. We love until we no longer feel like it. We love only when the other person does what we like. However, God's love for us is different. It is unconditional. And we image His love when we love our children unconditionally.

You might think, "But of course I love my children unconditionally!" Yet there are times we may unknowingly add conditions to our love. Our children may perceive and receive our love as conditional. They grow up thinking we love and accept them only when they behave, or when they look a certain way, or when they perform at a certain level.

> *God's love for us is unconditional. And we image His love when we love our children unconditionally.*

They learn this when we criticize them or point out their flaws. Our children learn to associate love with behavior when they see us treat them differently than or compare them to a sibling who outperforms them in some way. They also see love as conditional when we emphasize externals and when they observe us prioritizing what other people think about us—when we respond in anger because they embarrassed us in some way in front of others. They experience our love as conditional when we shame them for not measuring up.

Instead, our children need to know they are loved no matter what. Even when they fail. Even when they don't perform as other children. Even when they misbehave. As parents, we must communicate, both in word and in deed, that we love our children no matter what—anyway and always.

Love in Affection

One of the ways we show love and care for others is through our affection. We hug those we care about. We put our arm around the shoulder of one who is sad. We hold another's hand to show support and solidarity or for safety. Showing our love through touch is an important element to our relationship with our children. When a baby is first born, doctors encourage new parents to hold them skin to skin, for touch is an important element to an infant's thriving and to her attachment with her parents.

Lore Wilbert writes about the ministry of physical touch in her book, *Handle with Care*. She describes how touch can be either harming or healing. As we know, there's a lot of harmful touch in our world. The abuse children receive at the hands of their parents leaves lasting wounds. Yet, touch can also bring healing to the hurting. Wilbert points to Jesus' ministry of touch in the lives of those He ministered to such as the woman who bled for years, the little girl He raised from the dead, and the children He blessed: "when moved with compassion, Jesus *touched*."[7]

People vary on their levels of comfort with physical touch and our children will as well. Some children seem to be born huggers, others not so much. Some children with special needs might resist touch altogether. We don't have to smother our children with hugs if they don't prefer that. We can show affection by tousling the hair on their head, putting our arm around their shoulder, or patting them on the back. We can cover their hand and look them in the eye when we speak to them. We can high-five, and fist or elbow bump our teen who doesn't love hugs. We are embodied people and when we show love through proper touch, it provides comfort and care. It shows our love.

Love in Words

Words are important and speak to the heart and soul of another person. They can build up or tear down. They can comfort or cause pain. They can empower or weaken. They can guide or lead astray. "Gracious words are like a honeycomb, sweetness to the soul and health to the body" (Prov. 16:24). "Let no corrupting talk come out of your mouths, but only such as is good for building up, as fits the occasion, that it may give grace to those who hear" (Eph. 4:29).

God speaks to us through the Bible and His words give us life. Scripture tells us of God's great love for us in Christ. His words are active and alive. They have the power to dig deep into the marrow of our hearts, revealing secrets sins and bringing them to the light. His words sanctify and transform. They are our daily bread, which nourishes our very soul.

We image God when we use our words to build up and encourage our children. We do this when we tell them they are loved and treasured. We image Him when we use words to teach and train in righteousness and point, in wonder, to the beauty of all God has made. The next time you take a walk with your child, take a moment to pause and look at the butterfly flutter past or the curious insect crawling on the ground. Talk about how amazing God's creation is and that the same God who made the butterfly also made your child. How marvelous are His works! We also image God when we speak the truth and when we point them to the greatest truth of all: the good news of Jesus Christ.

Love in Action

Love isn't only words; it is also action. God doesn't only tell us He loves us, He proved it. The famous 1 Corinthians 13 passage not only tells us what love looks like; it also describes God's love for us. And like God, we show love when we are patient and kind. We demonstrate love when we are selfless and sacrificial, when we sacrifice time, energy, and resources for our children. We reveal our love when we are gentle and get down on their level, face-to-face, and listen to their cares. We demonstrate our love when we read the same story at bedtime each night; when we prepare meals for them; when we comfort their hurts; and when we play their favorite game. In all these ways and more, we love as the Father loves us.

My children increasingly realize the sacrifices my husband and I make for them. They know how much time we spend transporting them to school, games, or events. They've shown an awareness of how much it costs for them to have fun experiences or purchase material goods. I know this because they show their appreciation and express their gratitude for what we have done for them. They even thank me for picking up things they need from the store!

The investment you make of time and resources and energy on behalf of your children will pay dividends, both in your own heart and in that of your children. They will know your love for them and will see the Father's love for them through your actions.

Love for Good

In our family, when someone doesn't know how to do something, we don't just do the task for them, we show them how to do it. My husband often does this with our sons when an item breaks. Instead of repairing it himself, he'll teach them how to repair it. In this way, they've learned how to repair toilets, tools, cars, and other household items. Sometimes, if he doesn't know how to repair something, he'll encourage them to research it. I think my youngest is now an expert in setting up computer printers!

I do this as well when my children have to write a research

paper or essay for school. Rather than giving them the words to write, I help them think through the purpose of the paper, what they want to communicate, and various words to use to express their thoughts. We walk through the writing process together. Over time, they've grown increasingly confident in their writing.

I'm sure my children would much prefer that we did things the easy way. I imagine they would rather we just did things *for* them, but ultimately these lessons are for their good. They learn skills they need for the future. They are equipped to do things on their own. Likewise, God loves us for our good. He only does for us what we need most. Sometimes He doesn't give us what we ask for, but just what we need. He does so out of love for us so that we would grow and be reshaped to reflect Christ.

As parents, we too need to love our children for their good. This may mean not buying them the latest toy because we want them to appreciate the ones they have. It might mean not putting them on a team or in an activity that conflicts with time spent worshiping God. It's also for their good when we restrict them from certain television shows, movies, or video games because we know that once something is seen, it can't be unseen. Our love for our children is protective and sheltering. It is nurturing and encouraging. It equips and prepares.

A parent's love seeks the best for our children. That best doesn't always focus on the here and now, but also on the future. We love our children in light of eternity, desiring the best for their souls.

Love That Is Hard

Luke 15 begins with the Pharisees' grumbling words, "This man receives sinners and eats with them" (v. 2). Jesus responds with three parables: the lost sheep, lost coin, and the prodigal son. These parables speak to how God deals with our wayward and wandering ways. The parable of the son who demands his inheritance from his father and then leaves home and squanders it is a familiar one. He soon becomes impoverished and remembers the life he once had at home. He returns home in humility and his father stands there waiting. In fact, he's been waiting and watching all along. He receives him back, not as a servant, but as a cherished son. He doesn't shower him with shame for his actions, but with love and affection. He rejoices at his return and throws a party for all to celebrate.

Jesus did not teach this parable to instruct us in our parenting. It was to reveal the heart of God toward His children. It's a reminder of His lavish grace. And it's a reminder for us of how God parents us. In terms of our topic, when we encounter difficulty in parenting our children, we remember our own Father who is ever ready to receive us.

Indeed, there are times when loving our children is hard. Not that we don't want to love our children, but that we have to love them through hard times. Disabilities. Losses. Adolescent rebellion. Unrepentant sin. Devastating illness. Consequences for sin. We live in a fallen world where no one is left unaffected by sin's stain. Sometimes we have to love our children through difficult times, helping them navigate and endure painful circumstances. I've had to walk beside my children through various failures and losses. Oh, how I desperately wanted to remove their pain and sorrow! I felt helpless. All I could do was grieve with them. These are hard seasons as a parent. Even harder is when we walk beside them as they face consequences for sinful choices. In those times, wanting to protect and rescue them from those consequences may be our default. But often, those are the times when God's grace is most at work in their lives and in our own. Sometimes, we'll have to love our children from afar as they resist our love and seek their own way. All the while we'll be praying for the Lord to rescue them and bring them home.

When we face such hard love, we must remember the Father's love for us. He loved us when we hated Him. He rescued us when we didn't want rescue. He bought us at a price we could never repay. Love in a fallen world is never easy, but we don't love our children in our own strength. We rest in the fact that the Father loves them more than we ever could. His love is greater than our love. We must trust in His love to do what we can't do. "Love bears all things, believes all things, hopes all things, endures all things" (1 Cor. 13:7). We know this is true of our Father, may it also be true of us.

In all these ways and more, may we show the love of our good and perfect Father in the way we love our children. May they know the love of God through our love.

Questions for Discussion

1. Read 1 Corinthians 13:4–7. How does it describe God's perfect love for us?

2. Look at the list in this chapter describing God's love. What stands out to you most? What aspects of God's love do you need to learn more about?

3. Read Romans 12:9–21. The previous chapters in Romans tell us the indicatives of the gospel. These verses are the imperatives. Because God loved us in Christ, because we have the very Spirit of God living within us, how are we to treat others?

4. Why is it important to both tell and show our children that we love them?

5. Have you ever experienced conditional love from someone else? What was that like?

6. How have you experienced hard love with your children? What aspects of God's love for you can you remind yourself of in those moments?

7. How can you image the Father in how you love your children today?

A Parent's Prayer

Father in heaven, You are a God of love. Your love is perfect, right, and true. Whenever I consider the depths of Your love for me, I am left wonderstruck and amazed that You would love a sinner like me. As a parent, I want to love my children as You love me. I want Your love to shape my words and actions. Help me for I cannot do this apart from You. Holy Spirit, bear in me the fruit of love. Help me love sacrificially. Help me love as Jesus loved me.

In Jesus' name, amen.

CONCLUSION

At the start of this book, I talked about the questions we all have as parents. Most of those questions are "how?" questions. We want to know how to respond to our children, how to get them to stop a certain behavior, how to help them navigate difficult seasons of childhood. Throughout this book, I've attempted to scramble the letters and turn the question of "how?" to "who?": who God is as our Father shapes who we are as parents as we image Him to our children.

After going through these chapters, we can now return to the question of "how?" In the face of parenting dilemmas, we can now ask ourselves:

How can I image God to my child in this situation?

How can I image God to my child when she is exhausted and whining during a trip to the grocery store?

How can I image God to my teen who has difficulty navigating contemporary culture with wisdom?

How can I image God to my son who is struggling in school? With friendships?

How can I image God to my daughter who just failed at something important to her?

How can I image God when my child resists correction and whose heart is rebellious?

How can I image God when _____?

The truths of how God our Father parents us will guide us as we seek to answer questions such as these. The answers may not be easy; they may even be downright hard. But our Father models for us what it looks like to parent in the hard spaces, how to image the great love of God to our children, a love without conditions. God's love rescues. His love sacrifices. His love goes to great lengths. His love leaves the ninety-nine to seek and save the one who is lost. His love gave of His only Son to pay for our sins. His love ensures we endure to the end. To image this love to our children, we must keep the Father's love at the forefront of our own minds and hearts. His love for us shapes how we love our children.

As you close the pages of this book and seek to reflect the Father to your children, I wanted to leave you with some final encouragements.

Seek the Father in Prayer

A friend of mine and I often joke that we've given up on all parenting techniques but one: *prayer*. We joke about it because we both know how hard we tried to follow all the parenting methods and rules early in our motherhood. Eventually, we learned to trade our reliance on them and instead depend on the Lord in prayer. That's not to say that parenting methods and techniques are not useful or helpful; many of them are. Whatever parenting methods we seek to use must yield before the Lord for He is the One who rules over the results. We need to parent out of humble dependence on God. And we do so in prayer.

Seeking the Lord in prayer is essential for parents. We must bring our children before the throne of grace and seek God's help and grace in our time of need. For ourselves, we'll pray for strength, wisdom, perseverance, patience, and love. We'll also pray prayers of confession for our sin and seek the forgiveness Christ purchased for us. Because it is the Lord who changes hearts, we pray for His work in our children, saving and transforming them. As we pray, we bring to the Lord all the worries and cares we have for our children. And we pray the prayer that never fails: *Your will be done.*

May we all be quick to turn to our Father in prayer, seeking His help in all aspects of our parenting.

Seek the Wisdom of Other Image Bearers

Christian community plays an important role in our parenting. There are people in our churches who have walked the same parenting road we walk. They know the challenges we face each day with our children. They know the questions swirling around our minds every moment of the day. They know the heartache and tears we cry over our children. These seasoned parents have seen God answer prayer. They've learned from their mistakes. They've learned to image God in their own parenting. We need these brothers and sisters to speak into our own parenting. We need their wisdom and encouragement.

God gave us each other in the body of Christ to encourage and equip us to live for Him. The apostle Paul encouraged older members in the church to disciple and train the younger members (see Titus 2). May we seek out other parents to lead and guide us in our parenting. The ones we look to are those whose lives reveal that they abide in Christ. We see the fruit of the gospel in their lives. These brothers and sisters are less likely to give us a step-by-step guide to parenthood but will instead encourage us with biblical truth. They are honest about their own weaknesses and failures and testify to God's grace at work in them. They are good listeners who show compassion for our heartaches, sorrows, and fears. They are prayer warriors who pray with us as we pray for our children.

Let us pray for the Lord to bring parenting mentors in our lives who can encourage and exhort us to image God to our children. Let us also consider the ways we can mentor parents who are behind us in the journey, those who are in a parenting season we've already experienced.

Seek to Apply the Gospel of Grace

As fallen sinners, we all make mistakes in our parenting. We do and say things we regret. We don't image the Father to our children. We fail to be the parents we want to be. In these moments, turning to the gospel and appropriating the grace of Jesus Christ is the solution. Let's remind ourselves of the good news: that God the Father sent God the Son to incarnate in human flesh and live the life we could not live. Jesus Christ lived a perfect life, obeying God in all things. He faced all the temptations and sorrows of life in this fallen world, yet He never sinned. He then became the perfect sacrifice for our sin at the cross. He took on all our sin for us, paying our debt in full. Because He was sinless, the grave could not hold Him and He rose again from the dead, ensuring our own resurrection at the end of all things. He then gave us His Spirit to live within us, transforming us and making us new.

When we fail in our parenting, we're able to marvel once again at the gospel and bring our sins to the Lord and seek His forgiveness. We turn from those sins in repentance and ask the Lord for grace to begin again. Rinse and repeat. This is a habit we'll repeat throughout our lives until we are made perfect in glory.

Parents, may the truths of how the Father in heaven parents us strengthen and encourage you in your own parenting. May you always remember the great love of the Father for you in Christ. And may the Spirit of Christ enable you to mirror that love to your children.

Questions for Discussion

1. How has looking at the ways God parents you encouraged your heart?

2. How has it changed or impacted how you view your own parenting?

3. Out of all the ways we image God to our children, what is one way you'd like to grow and improve on in your own parenting?

4. Are there additional ways we can image God to our children that were not mentioned in the book?

5. Think of one or two people you can reach out to today to seek their parenting wisdom. Why do you choose them?

6. What are some areas of parenting you need to bring before the Lord in prayer?

7. How will you image the Father to your children today?

A Parent's Prayer

Father in heaven, the more I dwell on all the ways You parent me, I am amazed at Your great love. You are a perfect parent who only does what is good for me. Help me as I seek to image You to my children. I pray they would see You through me. Help me to depend on You and not rely on myself. Help me to seek Your wisdom and not my own. Help me to trust in Your grace. Please bring other parents into my life who can encourage me in this journey.

I pray all this in Jesus' name, amen.

ACKNOWLEDGMENTS

No book is ever written alone. Countless people impact the heart and life of a writer. That's why I always love writing acknowledgments to those who have prayed for and supported me in the process of writing a book.

I am thankful to Trillia Newbell for listening to my idea about this book and her excitement and belief in its message. We first met before either of us had yet published a book, and I love watching how the Lord has used her writing for His kingdom. It was a joy to work with her on this project, and I'm thankful for the opportunity. A big thank you also to Moody Publishers and the team for their belief in the project and their editorial work in getting it published. A big thanks to my literary agent, Don Gates. He is always so kind and encouraging and a joy to work with. I am thankful to have such a knowledgeable and trustworthy agent and am grateful for his labors on my behalf. And a huge thanks to Amanda Cleary Eastep and the editorial team at Moody for their work on editing and polishing this project. It was a joy to work with you!

Thanks to Dr. Stephen Estock at Committee on Discipleship Ministries. I appreciate his theological assistance and encouragement on this project.

To my two sons, Ethan and Ian, I am so proud to be your mom. Thank you for always praying for me. It is a joy to watch you grow into godly young men. Thanks also to my husband, George, of twenty-five years. It is a joy to journey through life together!

And to my friends and prayer warriors: Lisa Tarplee, Holly Mackle, Marilyn Southwick, Sarah Ivill, Amy Nelson, Maryanne Helms. Your faithful prayers for me are such an encouragement! To the women in my Tuesday evening Bible study and the members of my Life Group—thank you for praying for me and this project.

To my readers, I have enjoyed getting to know many of you. Thank you for reading and sharing with me your thoughtful words of encouragement!

NOTES

Chapter 1: In the Image of God

1. This chapter is not intended to thoroughly unpack every aspect of what it means to be an image bearer. There are many books written on this topic and I encourage you to study the topic further. A couple of places to start are *Made for More* by Hannah Anderson (Chicago: Moody, 2014) and *Freedom to Flourish, The Rest God Offers in the Purpose He Gives You* by Elizabeth Garn (Phillipsburg, N.J.: P&R Publishing, 2021).

2. Sinclair B. Ferguson, *Children of the Living God: Delighting in the Father's Love* (Edinburgh: Banner of Truth, 1989), 6.

3. Ibid., 7.

4. R. C. Sproul, *The Holiness of God* (Carol Stream, IL: Tyndale Publishing, 1985), 113.

5. Hannah Anderson, *Made for More: An Invitation to Live in God's Image* (Chicago: Moody, 2014), 36.

6. Arthur Pink, *The Attributes of God* (Grand Rapids: Baker Books, 1975), 9.

7. Jen Wilkin, "10 Things You Should Know about God's Incommunicable Attributes," Crossway, May 9, 2016, www.crossway.org/articles/10-things-you-should-know-about-gods-incommunicable-attributes/.

Chapter 2: God Our Father

1. Michael Erard, "The Mystery of Babies' First Words," *The Atlantic* (Atlantic Media Company, April 30, 2019), https://www.theatlantic.com/family/archive/2019/04/babies-first-words-babbling-or-actual-language/588289/.

2. J. I. Packer, *Knowing God* (Downers Grove, IL: InterVarsity Press, 1993), 203.

3. Sinclair B. Ferguson, *Children of the Living God: Delighting in the Father's Love* (Edinburgh: Banner of Truth, 1989), xi.

4. D. Blair Smith, "God the Father: A Name Is More Than a Metaphor," Tabletalk, September 19, 2018, https://tabletalkmagazine.com/posts/god-the-father-a-name-is-more-than-a-metaphor/.

5. D. Blair Smith, "God the Father and Our Adoption," Tabletalk, November 14, 2018, https://tabletalkmagazine.com/posts/god-the-father-and-our-adoption/.

6. J. I. Packer, *Knowing God*, 206.

7. Ibid., 207.

8. Twitter post by Tim Keller, February 23, 2015, https://twitter.com/timkellernyc/status/569890726349307904?lang=en

Chapter 3: God Is Consistent

1. Shelly Vaziri Flais MD, *Caring for Your School-Age Child: Ages 5–12* (New York: Bantam Books, 2018), 257–70.

2. This section is inspired by a blog post on christinafox.com titled "For Those Who Struggle with Change," https://www.christinafox.com/blog/2018/10/9/for-those-who-struggle-with-change?rq=For%20Those%20Who%20Struggle.

3. James K. A. Smith, *You Are What You Love: The Spiritual Power of Habit* (Grand Rapids: Brazos Press, 2016).

4. Ibid., 129.

5. Ibid., 130.

Chapter 4: God Provides Boundaries

1. R. C. Sproul, "Which Laws Apply?" Ligonier, May 1, 2017, www.ligonier.org/learn/articles/which-laws-apply/.

2. I'm thankful to Pastor Tim Locke for this insight.

Chapter 5: God Teaches and Trains Us

1. Trillia J. Newbell, *Sacred Endurance: Finding Grace and Strength for a Lasting Faith* (Downers Grove, IL: InterVarsity Press, 2019), 145.
2. Paul David Tripp, *Parenting: 14 Gospel Principles That Can Radically Change Your Family* (Wheaton, IL: Crossway, 2016), 178.
3. John Milton, "Of Education," https://www.dartmouth.edu/~milton/reading_room/of_education/text.shtml.

Chapter 6: God Disciplines Us

1. "Strong's Greek: 3809," Bible Hub, https://biblehub.com/greek/3809.htm.
2. Nancy Guthrie, *Hoping for Something Better* (Carol Stream, IL: Tyndale, 2007), 159.
3. Charles Spurgeon, "Chastisement," The Spurgeon Archive, https://archive.spurgeon.org/sermons/0048.php.
4. *Spirit of the Reformation Study Bible: New International Version* (Grand Rapids: Zondervan, 2003), 2001.
5. I'm thankful to Nancy Guthrie's summary of these three forms of suffering in her book *Hoping for Something Better* (Carol Stream, IL: Tyndale, 2007), 160–161.
6. Martin Luther: Ninety-five Theses (Latin)—CHRISTIAN Classics ethereal library, https://ccel.org/ccel/luther/theses/theses.ii.html.
7. Paul David Tripp, *Parenting*, 114.

Chapter 7: God Gives Us What We Need

1. Don Moen, "Jehovah Jireh," Give Thanks, track 6, Amazon Music Unlimited.
2. D. Martyn Lloyd-Jones, *Studies in the Sermon on the Mount* (Grand Rapids: Eerdmans Publishing, 1971), 383.
3. Ibid., 384.
4. Ibid., 390.
5. St. Augustine, *The Confessions of St. Augustine* (New York, NY: Barnes and Noble, 2003), 1.

Chapter 8: God Is Patient with His Children

1. Jonathan Edwards, *Charity and Its Fruits: Christian Love as Manifested in the Heart and Life* (Lawton, OK: Trumpet Press, 2014), 48.
2. Paul David Tripp, *Parenting*, 90.

Chapter 9: God Loves His Children

1. Gerald Bray, *Augustine on the Christian Life: Transformed by the Power of God* (Wheaton, IL: Crossway, 2015), 207.
2. Jonathan Edwards, 191.
3. Ibid.
4. Ibid.
5. Timeless Truths Free Online Library | books, sheet music. "And Can It Be?" And Can It Be? > Lyrics | Charles Wesley, https://library.time-lesstruths.org/music/And_Can_It_Be/.
6. Bryan Chapell, *I'll Love You Anyway and Always* (Wheaton, IL: Crossway, 2001).
7. Lore Ferguson Wilbert, *Handle with Care: How Jesus Redeems the Power of Touch in Life and Ministry* (Nashville: B&H Publishing, 2020), 18.